All-New Fire 7 User Guide

by Tom Edwards and Jenna Edwards

All-New Fire 7
User Guide

Newbie to Expert in 2 Hours!

by Tom Edwards & Jenna Edwards

Other Books By Tom & Jenna Edwards

250+ Best Kindle Fire HDX and HD Apps for the
New Kindle Fire Owner

Amazon Echo User Guide: Newbie to Expert in 1 Hour!

Chromecast User Guide: Newbie to Expert in 1 Hour!

Amazon Fire TV User Guide: Newbie to Expert in 1 Hour!

About this Fire 7 book

This book is a Fire 7 manual specifically concerned with the All-New Fire 7 inch tablet, Generation 5, released in 2015.

For other Amazon Fire tablets, including the Fire HD6 and the All-New Fire HD8 and HD10 please refer to our other books.

Contents

All-New Fire 7

Want the Latest Kindle Fire 7 App News?

Before we start, I just want to let you know about the FREE updates we offer all our customers. As you may know we are also the authors of **250+ Best Kindle Fire HDX and HD Apps** and we send out a monthly email with tips, tricks, news and reviews of five top apps for you to consider. These apps will help you get the best from your Fire tablet, so if you want to take advantage of our monthly recommendations then ...

Sign up for the updates here: *www.Lyntons.com/updates*

Don't worry; we hate spam as much as you do so we will never share your details with anyone.

Introduction

BEFORE WE START – IMPORTANT!

Throughout this book we recommend certain webpages that might be useful to you as a Fire tablet owner and user.

A lot of the webpages we recommend are on Amazon, and a typical Amazon web address might look something like this:

http://www.amazon.com/dp/B00DBYBNEE?_encoding=UTF8& camp=1789&creative=9325&linkCode=pf4&linkId= UPTTB3CK 67NSPERY&primeCampaignId=prime_assoc_ft

The link above takes you to the Amazon Prime sign-up page, but that's a lot of characters for you to type! So for the longer links we've used what they call a Link Prettifier to make the links shorter and easier to use.

In this example the shortened link is – *www.lyntons.com/USPrime* – if you type that into your browser, it will save you lots of typing time, but still take you straight to Amazon Prime....

WELCOME

When we first published our Fire tablet App review guide - **250+ Best Kindle Fire HDX and HD Apps for the New Kindle Fire Owner** - we added in a small bonus section which included a few tips and tricks for the new Kindle Fire user. We soon started receiving emails from customers asking for more of the same, so we published the first Kindle Fire User Guide in 2013. Since then Amazon have continued to upgrade both their Fire tablet hardware and operating system and each time we have updated our guides to reflect the latest new features. So what you hold in your hands today is, our complete and comprehensive, easy to understand guide to getting the most from the all new $49.99 (£49.99 in the UK) 7 inch Fire.

We've taken everything we know, scoured the official online Amazon guides, then read a whole lot more and put it all together for you here. What you are reading now is a user guide for both beginners and the tech savvy. This book contains the basics you need to navigate easily around your device but also the more advanced tips and tricks that will have you using your Fire tablet like a pro before you know it.

HOW TO USE THIS BOOK

Feel free to dip in and out of different chapters, but we would suggest reading this Fire 7 owner's manual from start to finish to get a clear overview of all the information contained. We have purposely kept this Fire 7 guide short, sweet and to the point so that you can consume it in a couple of hours and get straight on with enjoying your new Fire 7 tablet.

These Fire 7 instructions aim to answer any questions you might have about the Fire 7 5th generation tablet and the topics we cover include

- A general Fire 7 review

- Fire 7 Specs

- Walkthrough of the new Fire 7 Bellini OS5 operating system

- Fire 7 Setup instructions

- Fire 7 Storage

- Best apps for the Fire 7

- Fire 7 Family features

- How to download Fire 7 games, including Underground apps & games

- How to enjoy Fire 7 music and films

We also cover Fire 7 features like

- Fire 7 Second screen feature

- Fire 7 Mirroring feature

- Fire 7 FreeTime app for kids

- The Firefly app

- The new Fire 7 micro SD card and slot

- Fire 7 Bluetooth pairing

- Fire 7 Text to Speech

- Amazon Cloud Drive and Cloud Collections

- Trace Typing (Previously Swyping)

- Word Runner & Word Wise

- On Deck for Films & TV

If you have any other questions you can email us at ReachMe@ Lyntons.com, but this Fire 7 operation manual also has links to

- Fire 7 Customer Services

- Fire 7 Device Support (Mayday)

- Fire 7 Help videos

- Fire 7 Quick Start Guide

- Fire 7 Support

- Fire 7 FAQ's

So let's get started right at the beginning...

Just What is a Tablet?

As we're sure most of you know by now a tablet is a mobile computer operated by touchscreen that stores information on the Internet. This approach to data storage, called "the cloud," eliminates the need for an internal hard drive.

Tablets fill the gap between smartphones and laptops. A tablet has all of the functions of a smartphone and more, but the display size is three to four times as big. Navigating a tablet's touchscreen is similar to using a smartphone, which eliminates the need for a keyboard. Just like a smartphone, tablets can access the Internet and use applications ("apps") to make all kinds of online tasks easier, from checking the weather to balancing your checkbook to shopping at online stores like Amazon. The tablet's cloud-based storage cuts down on the weight and bulk so familiar to laptop owners. For many users, it offers the best of both worlds.

Although the $49.99 price makes the 7 inch Fire very attractive compared to other tablets on the market, the real selling point is the way it integrates effortlessly with Amazon's enormous online store. From its humble beginnings as an online bookstore, this ecommerce giant has grown into the world's largest retailer, and Amazon's digital content offerings have been a real success story too. From your Fire tablet you can choose from over 23 million media items, including books, movies, TV shows, apps and games, audiobooks, and music files. It's like holding the biggest library on the planet in the palm of your hand.

One of our favorite things about the Fire is that it's an Android-based tablet. Why is this so great? Because the Fire will run hundreds of free Android apps that you can download from the Amazon App Store, along with hundreds more third-party apps. It's true that the Android operating system has been altered by Amazon into a proprietary firmware for the Fire, so it won't run all of the Android apps in the Google Play app store. However, Amazon has built the device with a menu option to allow installation of non-Amazon apps, and we have been very satisfied with the results.

Please don't panic if, at this stage, all this tech jargon is a like a foreign language to you - by the end of this book you'll not think twice about using terms like "firmware" and "apps." **We wrote this book for complete beginners as well as Fire tablet veterans**. Our aim is not only to cover the how-to basics, but also to show you some of the lesser-known features of the Fire 7 that really make it fun to own.

New Fire 7 Specs

7" $49.99

- Screen size 7" (8.4" x 5.0 x 0.3")

- Resolution 1024 x 600 171 ppi

- One color: black

- Quad-core up to 1.3 GHz with 1 GB of RAM

- System: Fire OS 5 Bellini

- Mono speakers (no Dolby)

- Built-in microphone

- 8 GB storage, expandable by 128GB with microSD expansion

- Cameras: VGA front-facing camera, 2 MP rear facing camera with 720p HD video recording

- Single band Wi-Fi

- Battery life up to 7 hours

- Weighs 11 oz.

- Customer support: screen sharing, email, web, and phone

Fire Tablet Comparisons

So what's the difference between the new 7" Fire and the other more expensive HD models? Well frankly not that much given the super low price tag of $49.99. Basically the picture and sound quality are not as good on the low priced 7 inch Fire, so if you want the full HD experience with Dolby stereo sound then you'll be better off with the more expensive models.

The battery life is an hour less, the processor a tiny bit slower and the in-built cameras not as good as other models but again we feel that for most these differences won't be noticed. With the new 7" Fire Amazon have basically made tablet computers accessible to all!

1. GETTING STARTED

Controls and Battery

The power switch is a silver button located on the top right edge of the Fire tablet when you hold it in the "portrait" position, with the long edges in each hand and the short edges at the top and bottom.

You will see the lens of the front-facing camera at the top center of the device. Thanks to the auto-rotate feature, your Fire 7 will display correctly in any position shortly after you power it up.

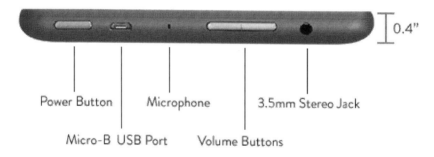

- To turn on your device, press and hold the power button for 2-3 seconds.

- To put it to sleep while the power is on, touch the power button.

- To wake up the device, touch the power button and then slide your finger up from the bottom of the touchscreen.

- To turn it off, press and hold the power button and follow the prompt to either shut down or cancel.

- To adjust the speaker volume, press either of the two silver buttons on the top left edge: left to decrease and right to increase.

- To plug in a pair of Fire tablet headphones, earbuds or external speakers, use the pin jack on the top edge.

You will need battery power to operate your Fire, tablet so it's best to start charging it up as soon as you take it out of its box for the first time. A micro-USB cable and USB power adapter are included in the box. Plug the full-size end of the cable into the power adapter unit. Plug the micro end of the cable into your 7 inch Fire's micro-USB port located just to the left of the power button.

When your device is powered up, a lightning bolt will display inside the battery icon at the top right of the touchscreen to let you know the battery is charging. (You can also charge your Fire's battery from a USB 2.0 port of your desktop or laptop computer or a USB hub, but it will take longer than using the charger.)

The Fire 7's battery is claimed to last about 7 hours on full charge during average use and we have found this to be accurate, unless we're doing a lot of downloads or other power-hungry tasks. Charging a completely dead battery through the USB cable and power adapter takes about 5 to 6 hours.

The Fire tablet is designed for you to hold it in either portrait or landscape orientation, which gives you great flexibility in adapting the device to the tasks you're using it for. Even better, it changes orientation automatically along with you when you rotate it 90 degrees. You can even use it upside down!

The Fire 7 uses a touchscreen, so you will be navigating through the menus with your fingertips. There are two touch commands you will be using often, so take a moment to practice them on the Fire touchscreen. Tapping means quickly touching your fingertip to an image on the screen, similar to clicking a mouse, and lifting it. You will tap once to select an item, such as a button, app icon, or block of text, and you will double tap to open an item. Swiping means sweeping your finger across the screen. You will swipe to scroll, to turn a page, or to open menus.

When you turn on your Fire 7 for the first time, it will automatically take you to an introductory demo screen that starts the registration process for the device. This screen will keep appearing until you register.

Setup and Registration

Your Fire tablet relies heavily on Amazon's cloud server, so your new device won't do much until you register it and link it with your Amazon user account. Registering allows you to wirelessly download your books, movies, games, apps, music, audiobooks, and other data that make your Fire tablet so much fun. Most new Fire owners will already have an Amazon account that they used to purchase their device, but if you received your Fire 7 as a gift and don't have an account, you can set one up during the registration steps.

First, turn on your Fire, 7 choose your language and tap *Continue*.

Next you will see a list of networks for connecting to the Internet. Your Fire tablet automatically scans for available wireless networks within range and lists them. Tap the network you want to use. Networks that require a password will have a lock symbol next to them, and you will need to know the password for that network (this is not the same as your Amazon account password).

If a wireless network password is required, the Fire's built-in onscreen keyboard will pop up so you can fill in the password box. The Shift key ⬆ on the keyboard is labeled with an upward arrow and lets you type capital letters. The ?1☺ key switches the keyboard layout between letters or numbers and symbols. When you tap this key, it will change the keyboard to numbers and symbols; tap it again to bring back the regular keyboard with letters.

When you have chosen a network, tap *Connect*. This network is now stored in your Fire, which will automatically find it and reconnect whenever it detects the signal.

Now that you are connected to the Internet, you will see a screen message that your Fire 7's system software is being downloaded and installed. This will take 15-20 minutes.

A Register Your Fire screen will appear. If you already have an Amazon account, type in the email address and password that you normally use to log in to that account. If you don't have an Amazon account, tap *Start here* under New to Amazon? to set up a new login and password with Amazon using the built-in keyboard.

Tap *Continue* and make sure the time zone displayed on your Fire tablet is the correct one.

If you see a Deregister button where the Register button should appear, you probably received your Fire 7 as a gift. Simply tap *Deregister* and go through the registration process above, using your own Amazon account information.

If you own other Fire devices, then setting up your new Fire tablet will give you the option to set it up with or without your content from a previous backup on another device. To transfer all of the content and settings from your other device to your new Fire tablet, tap *Choose Backup File*, tap the name of your previously registered device, and tap *Continue*. To set up your new Fire without adding your existing content, tap *Do Not Restore*.

If you've previously stored household profiles in your Family Library (see **Chapter 2**), an Import Profiles screen will appear. Tap the checkbox next to each profile to import it, or if you don't want to import it, uncheck the box by tapping it.

The Enable Location Services screen allows Amazon, some websites, and apps such as social media and maps to estimate your location. Tap *No Thanks* or *Enable* to set this service to your preference.

Next you will be prompted to link your Facebook, Twitter and Goodreads accounts with your Fire. You can do this now by clicking on the one or more of these social media links, entering your login and password for the social network, and tapping *Connect*. You can also skip this step for now by tapping *Continue*.

The Protect Your Fire screen appears next. This is an extended warranty protection plan for your Fire 7 device. If you're thinking of purchasing one of these plans, you don't need to do it during registration, but if you do buy it, it will take effect on the date your device was shipped to you no matter when you buy it. You can tap the *No Thanks* button to decline the plan, or tap the orange *Purchase* button to accept.

After registration, your Fire will run you through a very short tutorial about your device. Tap *Start* follow the orange prompts to move quickly through the tutorial, and tap *Exit* to end it, or simply tap *Exit* to skip the tutorial.

You will now see your "Home" screen. If you performed the Restore Your Fire step during the setup and registration process, then your Home screen will display any books and other media you have already purchased from Amazon. If you're tired of reading instructions and are anxious to get started actually using your Fire, tap one the content categories lined up across the top of your touch screen, such as books, apps or video, and tap a content icon to go ahead and open it!

Navigation

The starting point for all of your navigation on your Fire tablet is the Home screen. If you ever get lost while navigating your Fire, tap the small hollow circle icon at the bottom of your screen once or twice to go back to Home. If you can't see the circle, swipe toward the center of your screen from either the top or bottom edge.

Here is a detailed anatomy of the Home screen and how to find your way around it.

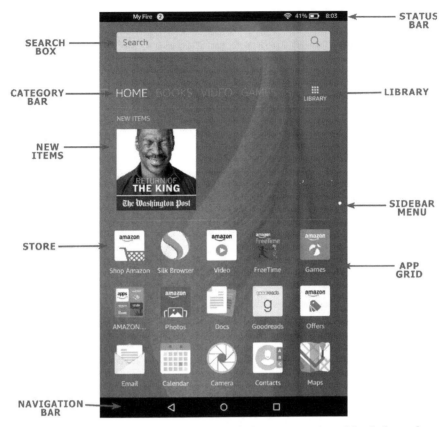

Status Bar: Across the very top of the screen is a black bar that displays information like the name of your device, the strength of your wireless network connection, the battery charge status, and the local time. You may see some other icons in this bar indicating your Fire tablet's settings. We will explain them in **Chapter 2**.

From left to right, the Status Bar's functions are:

My Fire **Device name:** the name of your Fire 7

② **Notifications:** messages sent to you by applications and games

✸ **Bluetooth:** indicates when Bluetooth signaling is activated

⊖ **Do not disturb:** shows when notifications and sounds are disabled

✈ **Airplane mode:** shows whether your device is connected to a wi-fi network

📶 **Wi-Fi indicator:** tells you how strong your Wi-Fi signal is.

51% 🔋 **Battery indicator:** displays how much battery power you have left

2:43 **Clock:** displays your local time

Search	Q

Search Box: This box, with a magnifying glass icon on the right, is always visible at the top of your screen below the Status Bar. It allows you to search the web, the Amazon store, or your Fire content library where the Amazon media items you buy are stored.

Tap this box and wait for the onscreen keyboard to appear. The onscreen keyboard pops up automatically for any task that requires text input.

To search by typing, type whatever you're looking for into the Search box. A list of choices will appear. Tap a word or phrase from this list of suggested search terms that appears in the drop-down menu below the Search box and tap the orange magnifying glass button in the lower right corner of the onscreen keyboard.

Your Fire 7 will first look on the internet for your Search box command and display the results on your screen. You can easily change your search to Amazon by tapping the center of the bar above the Search box, or by swiping right to left. To search all of your stored Fire materials with the same command, tap *My Stuff* on the right side of the bar above the Search box, or swipe right to left again.

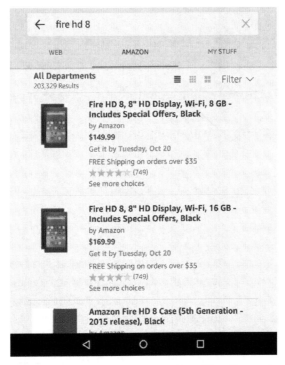

Category Bar: This display appears in white lettering across the top of your Fire tablet Home screen below the Search box. It's the gateway to the enormous world of digital content that awaits you as an Amazon user - over 38 million books, apps, games, movies, TV episodes, songs, and more. You can download and store thousands of Amazon media items on your Fire and use the Category Bar to access and organize them. You can also use it to access every single digital media item that you've ever purchased from Amazon, and of course to shop for even more content!

At the left end of the Category Bar are commands to display Recent (recently accessed content) and Home, followed by several content categories. These category sections make it easier for you to find specific types of digital media items in your Fire 7 downloads library, in your Amazon library online, or in Amazon's store.

From left to right, the categories are Books, Video, Games, Shop, Apps, Music, Audiobooks, and Newsstand (for magazines and newspapers). Swipe in either direction anywhere on the screen to display the next category. Tap any category in the Category Bar to open it, display its contents and select an item.

When you open a content category, you will see a magazine-style browsing menu with rows of content customized for you based on your previous purchases and search history in Amazon. If you already own Amazon content in the category you've selected, some of those selections will display across the top row. Below you'll see several rows of "recommended for you" content from Amazon's store for you to try or buy. Under the right side of most of these rows there's a "See more products" link in small blue text that you can tap to display even more content.

Library: Each content category has a Library icon 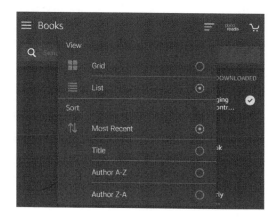 on the far right side of the Category Bar. Tap it to view the content you already own in that category. The All option displays all of your content that Amazon safely holds for you in your online library (called Amazon Cloud). The "Downloaded" option only displays your content that you've downloaded and stored on your Fire device.

Use the Search box to search your library within any content category on the Category Bar. Items that have been downloaded to your Fire tablet show a check mark in the corner of their thumbnail artwork. If you need to sort the way your library content displays, use the sort icon, which appears only in Library view at the top right of your screen and looks like a sheet of paper with lines written across it. The sort feature lets you switch your library items between grid view and list view, or change the display order.

Store: The second icon on the right side of the Category Bar in each content category is a shopping cart [STORE] and you can probably guess what that's for! Tap it to go to the Amazon Store section for that category, where you'll find recommended selections and several sub-categories that you can browse through. You'll also see recent releases, best sellers, and some special deals. You can use the Search box to find items in the Amazon Store with the onscreen keyboard. To shop in the entire Amazon store from your Fire, go back to the Home screen and tap *Store* in the Category Bar.

Sidebar Menu: There's a sidebar menu for each category that is only available in Library or Store view. To access the sidebar, tap any category in the Category Bar and tap the Library or Store icon. Swipe from left to right to reveal the sidebar, or tap the icon with three horizontal lines in the far upper left corner of the category next to its name [≡ Books]. The sidebar menu features a wealth of sort options, sub categories, and settings. Your Fire's Email and Calendar apps also have sidebar menus with the some of the same navigation as the content categories. Swipe right to left to hide the sidebar.

New Items: This section below the Category Bar displays randomly selected content that was recently delivered to your Fire tablet. These items can be quite random indeed, and their enormous icons really clutter up the touchscreen, so we prefer to remove them. To remove one or all New Items, press and hold that item. Tap *Remove from Home* to remove it from your home screen, or *Remove from Device* to delete it from your Fire. Deleting it from the screen display or your device won't remove it from your Amazon account, so you can always download it again.

App Grid: Apps are specialized software programs that perform specific jobs. The bottom half of your Home screen conveniently displays a grid of icons for every app installed on your Fire tablet. Swipe up or down to display all of the apps in your grid. Tap an app to open it. To uninstall an app you downloaded and installed on your Fire, press and hold its icon until a checkmark appears, and tap *Uninstall* in the top right corner of your screen. (Apps that come preinstalled on the Fire 7 can't be uninstalled.)

The App Grid lets you change the order of your app icons or drop them into folders. Press and drag an icon to change its position. Drag one app icon on top of another to place it into a folder and give the folder a name using the onscreen keyboard. Tap the yellow checkbox on the keyboard to save the folder name.

Navigation Bar: This is the black bar at the bottom of the Fire 7 touchscreen that helps you navigate between menu screens.

To go back to the previous screen you were using, tap the hollow arrow pointing to the left ◁, just as if you were using a web browser.

To go back to the Home screen, tap the hollow circle icon ◯ once or twice. To display your recently opened apps in reverse order, tap the hollow square icon ◻. Tap **Home** to hide them. To hide the onscreen keyboard, tap the hollow arrow pointing downward that appears whenever the keyboard is open.

If you don't see the Navigation Bar because your Fire tablet is in full screen view (for example, when you're reading a book), tap the center of the screen or swipe toward the center of your screen from the top or bottom edge.

Content Storage and Access

When you purchase and download digital content, such as an ebook, video, or app, from the Amazon Store, it is stored on your Fire as long there's enough space on its internal storage drive. Keep in mind that some of your Fire's storage space is taken up by its operating software, so not all of it will be available for storing your data.

The 7" Fire comes with 8GB of built-in data storage, but also has a microSD card slot, which expands the storage capacity up to an additional 128GB. You can use the microSD card to download and store videos, apps, games, and personal photos and videos. You can't use it to store books, audiobooks, web downloads from the Silk browser, or Email, so you'll have to use the Fire's built-in storage for those items.

The card slot is located on the upper right edge of the device when you hold it in the portrait position with the front-facing camera at the top. Carefully pry off the slot cover and turn it slightly to show the slot. With the top notch in the card facing upward, carefully slide the microSD card into the slot and push gently until it locks into place. Your Fire tablet will only work with certain types of cards. Amazon has provided a list of recommended cards that you can access from the Settings menu (see **Chapter 2**).

All About 'The Cloud': If you're new to the world of tablets, you might be confused by all the talk you've been hearing about "the cloud." To make things more confusing, Amazon has two cloud storage systems: the free storage you get as a customer for your Amazon content in Amazon Cloud, and Amazon Cloud Drive, which is a paid service for non-Amazon content. These are really two separate items, so let's try to clear up any confusion!

Amazon Cloud: Tablets like the Fire 7 have much less internal data storage than a laptop or desktop computer, so they store most of their content online. Online data storage is called "the cloud" in tech lingo, and Amazon maintains its own cloud to store customers' digital content. Space in your Amazon Cloud library account is free and unlimited, as long as you only fill it with digital stuff you purchase from Amazon.

The great thing about Amazon Cloud is that you can free up internal storage on your Fire tablet at any time by deleting from your device any content you purchased from Amazon, knowing that Amazon will always keep a copy for you to download again at any time. To download content from your Amazon Cloud library to your Fire, simply tap the appropriate content category in the Category Bar, tap *Library*, and tap the item's icon to download the file again.

Amazon Cloud Drive: This data storage service is a paid product that blends seamlessly with from your free Amazon Cloud account on your Fire. 7 Amazon Cloud Drive lets you store non-Amazon digital content that you already own, such as your personal photos, MP3 music files, home videos, etc. See **Chapter 8** for more info on how to use the Cloud Drive Desktop Application.

Cloud Collections: This Fire tablet feature lets you assemble your books, apps, games, audiobooks, and personal documents into one or more customized groups and store them in your Amazon Cloud library. Cloud Collections can be synced across all Amazon devices that support this feature. You can add as many items as you would like to each collection. Currently this feature doesn't support adding videos, music, newspapers, magazines, or photos.

To create a new Cloud Collection, tap any eligible content category in the Category Bar, tap the *Library* or *Store* icon, swipe left to display the sidebar menu, and tap *Collections*. Tap the + *icon* at the top right of the screen. Name the collection using the onscreen keyboard and tap *Create*. Tap one or more items you want to add to your collection and tap *Add* in the upper right corner.

To access a collection, display the sidebar menu in Library or Store view for any content category by swiping left to right, and tap *Collections*. Tap the icon for the collection you want to view.

To add a title to one or more Cloud Collections, tap the *Library* icon in any content category. Press and hold an item and tap the + *icon* in the upper right corner. Tap the checkbox next to each collection you want to add the item to and tap *OK*.

To rename a collection, press and hold the collection icon and tap the pencil icon in the top right corner. Type the new collection name into the field and tap *Rename*. To delete an item from a collection, open the collection, press and hold the icon, and tap the *"minus"* icon in the top right corner. Deleting the item from the collection won't delete the item from your device.

To delete a collection, press and hold the collection icon and tap the trash can icon. This will delete the collection as a group but will not delete any of the items that made up the collection.

2. CUSTOMIZING YOUR SETTINGS

Your Fire has been programmed to automatically give you the best settings, but you can change them to your liking to match how you use your device. Although you won't be changing them often, they can make your navigation experience faster and less frustrating. The Fire tablet is small enough to go wherever you go, so we encourage you to make your Fire display uniquely you!

One very important function you should take care of right away is setting a PIN or password for your lock screen so no one can access your Amazon account and stored credit card information without your consent. Tap the **Settings** icon in the App Grid, scroll down to the Personal section, and tap **Security**. Tap **Lock Screen Passcode** and select whether you want to use a 4-digit numeric PIN, or a secure password. Confirm your PIN or password and tap **Finish**. Be sure to write down your PIN or password in a secure location for safekeeping.

Quick Settings Menu

This menu is hidden on your Home screen until you swipe down from the top edge of the screen to make it visible. From here you can easily adjust the settings you're most likely to use. To hide it again, swipe upward toward the top edge of the screen. Some of these menu items have sub-menus. To go back to the previous menu from within any sub-menu, tap the left arrow in the Navigation Bar at the bottom of the screen.

Brightness: Use the slider to adjust screen brightness.

Wireless: Detect and connect to or disconnect from a list of nearby wireless networks. Your Fire tablet will automatically connect to the network you most recently used if it's available.

Airplane Mode: Tap the airplane icon to quickly connect and disconnect from a wi-fi network. We turn off our wireless connection whenever we're not using it to save the Fire's battery life.

Bluetooth: Tap the Bluetooth symbol and tap the switch icon to make your 7 inch Fire discoverable by a Bluetooth accessory or device. The Fire supports some wireless Bluetooth devices, including an external keyboard, mouse, speakers, or headset. It does not officially support Bluetooth microphones or headsets with a built-in microphone, but some of these may work on your device anyway.

Do Not Disturb: Tap to quickly hide notifications and mute notification sounds.

Firefly: Opens the Firefly app on supported devices to scan and identify physical products and find more details or purchasing information about them. You can also use Firefly to listen to audio in order to identify movies, TV shows, and music, and even to identify some artwork.

Help: Lists the on-device Help options and Amazon Customer Service contact information. You can find more information about Amazon's support services in **Chapter 9**.

Auto-Rotate: Enables screen rotation or locks the device in the portrait mode.

Settings: Tap to access a long (very long!) list of additional settings for your Fire tablet. (This sub-menu is also accessible by tapping the *Settings icon* in the App Grid.) To make things less confusing for you, we cover this menu in a separate section below.

The Settings Menu

The Settings menu in the lower right corner of the Quick Settings menu offers you extra options that you may want to adjust to suit how you use your Fire 7, including things like customizing the Keyboard function and setting up Parental Controls. Here is a detailed explanation of each item on the Settings menu, as they appear from top to bottom on your Fire. The setting menu is a very long page so we have broken it up into three separate images.

Settings Image 1

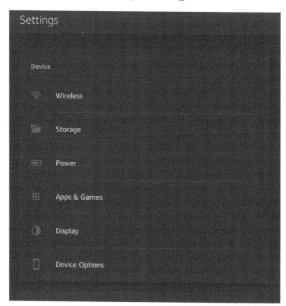

Wireless: This is the same sub menu that appears when you tap *Wireless* directly from the Quick Settings menu.

Storage: This sub menu lets you quickly free up storage space by deleting items from your 7 inch Fire that you haven't recently used. These items will still be archived in your Amazon Cloud library. You can also use this menu to check how much internal storage you have left on your Fire, or to browse the Amazon Store for a recommended microSD card.

Power: Conserve battery life by using this sub menu to manage functions that drain your Fire 7 battery faster. We recommend enabling Automatic Smart Suspend, which turns off your wireless connection when you aren't using your device.

Apps & Games: This sub menu lets you manage your apps and see which ones are running. From here you can change an app's notification settings, delete old data that an app has stored on your Fire's hard drive to free up memory space, and change the way an app interacts with your other content libraries. You also may wish to disable Collect App Usage Data, which Amazon turns on by default to keep track of how often and how long you use your downloaded apps.

Display: This sub menu allows you to change your screen brightness and adjust the timeout period before the screen goes into lock mode if you don't touch it. You can also customize your Fire tablet touchscreen by adding a background photo. From the Display sub menu tap *Wallpaper* and select a photo from your photo library to display. Display Mirroring is another selection in the Display sub menu. It allows you to mirror your Fire display to compatible TV's and other media streaming devices, or an HDMI dongle such as the Fire TV Stick or Google Chromecast.

Device Options: This sub menu lets you check your Fire's serial number, see if its firmware version is up to date, back up your device, monitor the battery charge level, and change your time zone. You can also turn on the Find Your Tablet to enable Location Based Services so you can find your Fire remotely - not a bad idea in case your device is ever stolen.

The last option on the Device menu is **Reset to Factory Defaults**. This item wipes your Fire's hard drive completely clean in case you want to sell or give away the device - or if you forget your password and have to reset it (see **Chapter 9**). Treat this menu option with all due respect!

My Account: This sub menu controls how your Fire 7 talks to your Amazon account. The e-mail address you see under this option is your

Amazon account e-mail that you used earlier to register your Fire. If you want to deregister your device so you can sell it or give it away, tap the **Deregister** button. (To erase all content from your Fire's storage drive, use the Device Options sub menu.) You can also change some general email settings from this menu, manage Amazon account information and payment options, control your Prime membership, and manage how your Fire 7 connects with Twitter, Facebook, and Goodreads if you skipped this step when you registered.

Settings Image 2

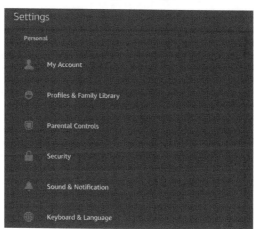

Profiles and Family Library: One Fire device can support unique profiles for up to 2 adults and 4 children. Users can select their own profile from the lock screen and have their own customized home screen, collections, preferences, apps, and content. This option lets each member of your family have a personalized experience on your 7 inch Fire. Prime members can also share Prime benefits with other members of their household.

Parental Controls: If you want to restrict what other users can see on your Fire (and if, like us, you have kids who love the Fire as much as you do, then the answer is going to be yes!), tap **Parental Controls** in the Settings menu and again in the sub-menu. You will be prompted to enter a password. (It should be different from the one you use for the lock screen of your Fire tablet, and one that your kids are unlikely to guess!) *Confirm* and tap *Finish*. Important: be sure to write down your parental password and store it in a safe place. (See **Chapter 9** for what to do if you lose your password.)

Setting your parental controls password brings up a menu where you can give children and anyone else who doesn't have the password the ability to use only the Fire features you want them to use. You can use this menu to lock them out of the following functions on your Fire:

• Silk web browser

• Social networks

• Camera

• Amazon Maps app

• Email, Contacts, and Calendar apps

• Firefly app

• All Amazon purchases

• Amazon Video

• Specific content categories (for example, Books or Apps)

• Wireless network

• Location-based services

If you want to change any of these Parental Controls later on, or change your password, you will need to re-enter your password to unlock this menu. Parents should also check out **Chapter 4** for information about Amazon's Free Time app and content delivery program for kids.

Security: Here is where you set a password for your lock screen as we explain above. This is very important because your Fire is hooked up to your Amazon account and one-click purchasing. When your Fire powers up or goes into timeout, swipe the lock icon up from the bottom of your screen and enter your password to unlock it. Important: be sure to write down your password and store it in a safe place. (See **Chapter 9** for what to do if you lose your password.)

Another setting in the Security sub menu is Apps from Unknown Sources. If you want to install apps that aren't available in the Amazon store, you need to tap *On* for this option. (See **Chapter 4** for more information.)

Sound & Notification: This sub menu allows you to set which apps you want to receive notifications from - for example, whether you want your Calendar app to put a notification in your status bar to remind you of an appointment. The Do Not Disturb sub menu is identical to the one you can access directly from the Quick Settings menu to turn off notifications. You can also adjust your Fire tablet's speaker volume using the slider bar on this sub menu if you don't want to use the buttons on the outside of the case.

Keyboard & Language: You can change the language setting on your Fire 7 by tapping *Language* from this sub menu and selecting your preferred language from the list. To customize the onscreen keyboard, tap *Fire Keyboard* and choose from several options. You can turn automatic capitalization and auto-correction on or off, and you can choose whether to enable Check Spelling to show suggested corrections and highlight possible misspellings.

You can also enable Next Word Prediction to predict words based on previously entered text, enable Trace Typing, and download a different keyboard language. Finally, you can also turn on the Keyboard Sounds to get the effect of a mechanical keyboard. We both use this feature even though we feel a bit silly about it - it seems to help with the accuracy of our typing. Kids who grow up using only a touchscreen will wonder why this option even exists!

Sync Device: Tap to connect your Fire to your Amazon Cloud library and make sure all of the digital content you've ever purchased from Amazon is displayed in your Fire 7's content library menus. Sync also updates your Amazon books, movies, music, and other data that you've downloaded to your device's storage drive.

Settings Image 3

Help: This is the same sub menu that appears when you tap *Help* directly from the Quick Settings menu.

Accessibility: This sub menu allows you to adjust your Fire for enhanced vision and hearing capabilities. The Fire features Voice View natural language text-to-speech voice software to provide spoken feedback when you touch the screen and adjust the reading speed slower or faster. There's closed captioning for videos that have it, and a screen magnification command. The Voice View feature gives several accessibility shortcuts to help you navigate the touchscreen. These features are especially useful for people with disabilities.

Legal & Compliance: This sub menu has no user commands.

About Lockscreen Advertising

Part of the buzz when the first Kindle Fire was released concerned Amazon advertising. For a discount ($15 in late 2015), you can buy a Fire that displays advertising. (Or, put another way, for an extra fee you can buy a Fire with no ads.) We don't mind the ads. At least for now, they're unobtrusive, and if Amazon gets more aggressive about displaying them in the future, there's always the option of paying the fee to remove them later on.

Currently, the advertising appears on the lockscreen when the device is locked. To unsubscribe from the Sponsored Lockscreen, you will need to go to the Amazon store from either the Fire Silk browser, or from the browser of your desktop computer.

Log in to your Amazon account, tap the small inverted triangle next to Your Account on the top navigation bar, and select *Manage Your Content and Devices* from the drop-down menu. Click the *Devices tab*, choose your device, scroll down to *Special Offers*, and click *Edit*. A window will pop up displaying the price to unsubscribe. From here it's just like making any other Amazon purchase. (Note that the Shop Amazon app on your Fire won't work for this process.)

If you want to see all of your offers at once, tap the *Amazon Offers app* on the App Grid. This app also lets you set your lockscreen offers to personalize based on your purchase and search history, and to filter lockscreen offers for inappropriate content.

Using the Fire 7 Keyboard

One of the more interesting aspects of tablet technology is the fact that - mainly because of the limited space the screen affords - the onscreen keyboards are not fixed, but are dynamic, with the ability to change format depending on what you are typing. This means that the keyboard can do things like switch from letters to numbers and symbols (to do this on the Fire keyboard tap the numbers and symbols key ?1☺), or offer the user the new fluid typing technology such as Trace Typing (see below).

The keyboard interface is fairly self-explanatory for anyone who is familiar with the traditional Qwerty keyboard, but here are a couple of short cuts that may prove useful. Please note that if you prefer to use the Trace Typing mode then there are some different shortcut commands that we go through below.

Delete: delete the character before the cursor by tapping the *delete key*, which is the back arrow with the "x" inside in the lower right corner of the onscreen keyboard. To delete all, hold down the *delete key*.

Change keyboard language: Tap and hold the space button to choose from a variety of different languages, including French, Spanish and Japanese.

Hidden capitals lock: Double tap or tap and hold the *Shift key* to keep letters in capital form. Tap *Shift* again at the end when you want to unlock this function.

Quick access to numbers and symbols: When the keyboard is in letters format you will see small numbers or symbols in the corner of each letter button. Tap and hold on the letter key for a second and you will see an orange button with the number or symbol. Lift your finger off the letter button and that number or symbol will automatically be inserted into your text.

Quick new sentence: Double tap the space bar at the end of a sentence to get a period followed by a single space and capitalization of the next word.

Punctuation shortcut: Tap and hold the period key to bring up a few other useful punctuation keys.

Dot com button: When you're using the Silk browser, or using email, and you type in a web or email address, a ".com" button appears on the keyboard next to the period button, and if you tap and hold on this button other domain name extensions appear (".org", ".net", etc).

Advanced symbols: When the keyboard is in numbers and symbols format, the shift button changes to a ~\< key - tap on this to access less usual symbols such as foreign currency symbols, square brackets, percentage mark etc.

Editing shortcut: Tap on an empty area near your text to access an Edit tool (which looks like an arrow tab). Tap on this tool and drag it to the place in the text that you want to edit then lift your finger to release the tool and edit the section. When you're done, tap the edited section again to see the Edit tool - drag to the end of your text and release it to exit the function.

Cut, copy and paste: Tap and hold on a word to access and choose cut, copy or paste options - select more words by sliding the highlight arrows. To paste your copied or cut text, tap and hold on the screen in the place you want to add the text and then choose the paste option.

Using Trace Typing with the Fire Keyboard

We never quite mastered the art of two-fingered typing, but we do like Trace Typing (previously called "Swype") ...provided you lift your finger off the keyboard between traces.

It offers all kinds of shortcuts to make using the onscreen keyboard more efficient. It isn't an app, so you don't have to do anything special to use it. It does have a learning curve, but Amazon has claimed that users can reach speeds of over 50 words per minute. (We're still working on that!)

Enable Trace Typing from the Keyboard & Language sub menu in the Settings menu. You Trace Type a word by tracing a line with your finger across the letter keys in that word. The critical step is lifting your finger when you reach the last letter of the word.

You don't have to lift your finger and skip over the letters you don't want in the middle of the word - the Fire tablet does that for you by detecting all the possible words that could be formed from the line you traced and listing them across the top of the keyboard display. Touch the correct word and it will insert into your text. It also automatically enters spaces between words, provided you lift your finger off the keyboard between traces.

3. USING THE INTERNET

If you have registered your Fire tablet, then you already have set up wireless access for it (see **Chapter 1**) through a Wi-Fi hotspot. You can manage your wireless networks from the Quick Settings Menu. Swipe downward from the top of your Fire screen and tap the Wireless icon to join a Wi-Fi network, switch networks, or disconnect wireless access to make your battery last longer.

Setting Up Email, Calendar, and Contacts

These three functions come as three separate apps on your Fire that are programmed to sync with each other. The Email app needs a bit of setup work before you can sync it with the other two applications. We're really pleased with the Fire 7's Email app that syncs with web-based email services like Gmail and Yahoo with just a few taps.

Setting Up Email: It's good to start by registering your Amazon account login email as your Fire's default email account, although you can start with any email account. Begin by tapping the Fire Email app from the Apps Grid on the Home screen. You will see the *Add Account* screen. Enter your email address using the onscreen keyboard and tap *Next*. Fill in your password and tap *Sign In*. Click *Accept* on the next screen to allow the Fire Email app access to your account, and wait for it to check your settings and register your email address. Your device will walk you through a short tutorial on how to use the Email app.

Now tap *Inbox* in the sidebar menu to see your email in that account. The app will populate your Fire Calendar and Contacts apps at the same time. Repeat the Add Account process if you want to add your other email accounts.

Fire's Email app easily links with Google Gmail, Yahoo, Hotmail, and other web-hosted email services and will also import your contacts and calendar from these accounts.

Linking to email providers that Fire doesn't recognize, such as your local broadband service, or your own domain name, is a bit more involved, but we were successful on the first try by opening our email client software on our computer, opening the Accounts menu, and duplicating the settings in our Fire Email app.

After entering your email address and password, the Fire Email app will ask you to choose whether to store this email as a POP3, IMAP, or Microsoft Exchange account. POP3 access downloads all of your emails to your device, while IMAP leaves them on your email provider's servers, allowing you to view all of your mail on any device you own. (Gmail also offers you the choice of accessing it as a POP3 or IMAP account, but you will need to configure this in Gmail through your web browser.)

Some users will need to set up an email account using Microsoft Exchange, especially if they need to check their workplace email account. Exchange might force you to set a password for your Fire lockscreen due to Microsoft's security requirements, but this is something you should do anyway (see **Chapter 2**). Once you've chosen which type of account you want to add, follow the Email app prompts to finish setting it up. Refer to your computer's email client software account settings as a guide, or use your Internet provider's support system.

Changing Your Email Settings: Once you've added your email accounts, you can change the settings from within the Email app by swiping from left to right to display the sidebar menu. You might need to scroll down on the sidebar to find the app's Settings menu. This menu lets you create separate settings for each of your email accounts and set some global options for all of your accounts, such as whether to display embedded images, automatically download attachments, and include the original message in your reply.

Within individual email accounts, you can choose whether to check your email manually, or automatically at a certain time interval. You can customize each email account display name, which is what shows up in the "From" column when other people get email from you, and you can create an account-specific signature for your messages if you like. You should also name the email account you're setting up on the Fire so you can tell it apart from any other email accounts you set up on the device. The email applications menu also lets you specify how many messages you want the Fire to store on its internal storage drive.

The Settings menu in the sidebar also lets you add more accounts and change your default email account.

You can also remove an existing email account - just remember that removing an email account also removes all stored emails, contacts, and calendars.

Using the Email App: We were pleased to find that the Fire email app has all the familiar functions of other email programs we have used on our desktop and laptop computers. The app looks a bit different, but the commands are the same.

When you swipe from left to right, the Email app displays an Unread folder for your email accounts at the top of the sidebar menu, plus an Inbox folder and an Unread folder for each separate email account.

To show more folders, choose *Show Folders* for the account you want. (Gmail accounts will say Show Labels instead, since they don't use folders.) You can tap each folder's icon to look at its contents. Tap a single message to open it and read it.

The Email app checks your messages automatically at the interval you specified in the app's Settings menu. To check your email manually, go to the inbox screen and swipe downward. To read a message, tap its subject line in your inbox. If you want to add the sender to your contacts, tap the sender's image in the email and tap **Add to Contacts**. You can also tap **Set as VIP** to add the sender to a separate list of VIP Contacts in the sidebar menu for quick reference.

If you want to read your messages from other devices, such as your smartphone or computer, then you might need to change some settings.

IMAP accounts, such as Gmail, Yahoo and Hotmail, automatically leave your messages on their servers until you delete them. POP3 accounts are a different story - your Fire tablet defaults to leaving messages on your POP3 server, but because POP3 servers don't automatically store your mail, it's a good idea to check the Incoming Settings sub menu for these email accounts to make sure!

To send a message, go to the lower-right corner of your Inbox screen and tap the pencil icon in the round blue circle ✐. Type an email address in the To line. If that person is already on your list of contacts, the app will suggest an address. To add a new address to your contacts, tap the *"+" icon* to bring up Contacts and save it. Now type in a subject line and type your message. Tap the **Send arrow** icon, or **Cancel** to delete.

To reply to or forward an open message, tap **Respond** and choose from **Reply**, **Reply All**, or **Forward**. Enter a To address and subject line, type your message, and tap **Send**.

To add an attachment to an outgoing email, tap the paper clip icon in the upper right corner and then tap **Attach a Photo, Attach a File**, or **Capture a Photo**. The Fire email app lets you attach documents, photos, and even music tracks you purchase from Amazon and download to your device.

To download or open an attachment to an email you have received, view the message, tap the **download icon**, and tap and hold the attachment to open or save it. The attachment will save to your Documents library, which you can access from the Documents app in the App Grid.

To delete a message, tap the checkbox next to any message you want to delete; then tap the **Delete** trashcan icon. To save a draft of a message, tap the menu icon with three vertical dots in the upper right corner and tap **Save Draft**. Tap **Discard Draft** using the same icon to delete.

To add a custom signature, swipe left to right to open the sidebar menu, and then tap on your email account; you'll then see a Signature option where you can add your personal sign-off message/ signature.

Calendar: The Fire tablet's Calendar app looks and acts like any other standard calendar software, but it has one extra-cool feature: it can sync with many online calendars such as Google Calendar and Yahoo Calendar. This allows you to work from the same calendar no matter which device you are using. Some Windows Live accounts are not supported by the app.

To open the Calendar app, find and tap it in the Apps Grid.

Contacts: This address book app syncs with your online email accounts. To open it, find and tap it in the Apps Grid. You can import and export your contacts to or from another app or change the way the app sorts names by tapping the menu icon with three vertical dots in the upper right corner. Tap **Import/Export**, or tap **Settings** to set your Contacts options.

Using the Fire Silk Browser

Amazon's Silk browser comes pre-installed on the Fire 7. Part of this browser's functioning takes place on Amazon's enormous Cloud Drive, which works in tandem with your Fire tablet to make your web surfing a smooth ride.

Open the browser from the Home screen by tapping the *Silk Browser* icon from the Apps Grid.

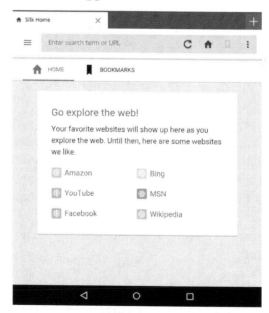

The browser window will open with a starter screen that displays Amazon as a default bookmark. To get started with browsing, type a search term or web address into the Search box at the top of the screen.

The layout is fairly intuitive for anyone who uses the Internet, with tabbed browsing, bookmarks, and browsing history. The only thing that initially confused us is that the Back arrow is at the bottom of the browser window, in the Navigation Bar, instead of at the top.

Basic Search: Silk combines the Search box with the web address box, similar to Google Chrome. To search the web, tap the **Search box** to bring up the onscreen keyboard.

Type your search term into the box and tap the big orange arrow key at the bottom right of the keyboard to get your search results. Tap a result to open that web page. You can also type a website address directly into box, or type in a partial address and choose from the list of options that the browser brings up.

Tabbed Browsing: Tap the **"+" key** in the upper right corner of the browser window if you want to open a new tab to browse in. To open a link in a new tab on an existing search result or web page without leaving that page, tap and hold the link and choose **Open in New Tab** from the pop-up menu.

To close a tab, tap the **X** in the right corner of the tab. To display the Starter screen when the Silk browser is already open, close each open browser tab by tapping the **X**, or tap the **"+" key** to open a blank tab.

Bookmark a Page: Tap the ribbon icon in the upper right corner of the Search box to bookmark a page. To view your bookmarks, swipe from left to right to display the sidebar menu and tap **Bookmarks**. To visit a bookmarked page, tap its listing. To delete a bookmark, tap and hold its listing, tap **Remove bookmark** on the pop-up menu, and tap **Remove.**

View Your Browser History: Swipe from left to right and tap **History** in the sidebar menu to see a list of sites you have visited in the past seven days. If you want to delete your history, tap the **trash can icon** in the upper right corner of the History menu and check the types of history you want to delete.

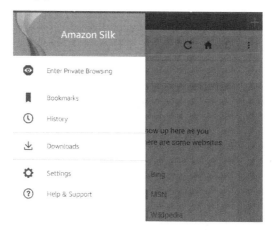

Personalize Your Browser: Swipe from left to right and choose *Settings* to bring up a number of customization options for the Silk browser. Most of the options will be familiar to you from other browsers, such as blocking pop-up windows, clearing the cache, and managing cookies.

Many websites have versions designed for mobile browsing. Their looks and functionality are improving, but we still feel that the Fire screen is big enough to handle the desktop versions of sites like Facebook and CNN.

To choose a different viewing option, tap the menu icon with three vertical dots on the right side of the search box and toggle between *Request Desktop Site* or *Request Mobile Site*. Note that the Silk browser doesn't support Flash streaming video, but sometimes you can solve this problem by switching to Mobile View. Some popular websites may have their own apps that allow you to view their video content on the Silk browser.

One personalization feature we use often is enlarging or reducing the browser page display magnification. There are two ways to do this. You can double tap the page to enlarge it and double tap it again to reduce it. The other method is "pinching": place two fingers on the touchscreen and spread them apart to enlarge, or pull them together to reduce. Note that you'll need to wait for the page to finish loading before either of these methods will work.

Another very cool feature we use on the Fire tablet is the ability to share any web page in an email directly from the Silk Browser. Tap the menu icon with three vertical dots in the search bar with the page open and tap the Share option on the menu. It's a good way to share your discoveries on the web with friends and professional contacts who don't use Twitter or Facebook.

Using Other Search Engines: The Fire Silk browser defaults to the Bing search engine, but if you prefer to use Google, or Yahoo, you can change the default search engine setting. Swipe from left to right, tap **Settings**, and tap **Search Engine** to choose your new default search engine.

Shopping on Your Fire Tablet

The Fire device makes shopping on Amazon incredibly easy, which is yet another smart marketing strategy for them. You can shop for digital content from within each content category on your device, or you can use the Amazon shopping app to shop the entire Amazon website at once. For digital content purchases from Amazon, you first must enable a 1-Click Payment Method in your Amazon account. (This is true even if you are downloading free content or apps.)

Setting Up 1-Click Payment: You will need a credit card on file with Amazon to complete this task. Open the Settings menu from the Apps Grid, tap **My Account**, tap **Amazon Account Settings**, and tap **Payment Options**. Log in to your Amazon account and tap the **Edit link** to change your 1-Click Payment options.

Shopping for Digital Content: Each of the content categories on the Fire Home screen has its own app for accessing the Amazon store. Pick a content category, tap **Store**, and a new screen will open to take you on a shopping spree in that content category. For example, if you go to the Home screen, tap **Apps**, and tap **Store**, the Amazon App Store will load on your screen.

The main page of each store app will feature freebies and special sale items, with suggestions for items you might want to buy based on your past search and purchase history with Amazon. There is an option to look at Best Sellers, and an option for New Releases. Each store's main page also includes a Search box. If you already know what you want to buy, tap the Search box to bring up the onscreen keyboard and type in the name of your item. Click the Buy button to purchase the item with your 1-Click Payment method and download it to your Fire tablet.

If you don't want to buy an item right away, you can tap the More Options button and tap Add to Wish List so you can come back to it later. To see your Wish List, swipe from left to right and tap Wish List to bring up your list.

Shopping on Amazon: There are two ways to shop on the entire Amazon site from your Fire. The first way is to go to the Home screen and tap *Shop* in the Category Bar. This option appears in the center of the Category Bar, and we don't think this is any accident!

The other way to shop is to tap the *Shop Amazon app* in the Apps Grid. Either way, the user experience is very similar to shopping on Amazon from your desktop or laptop computer.

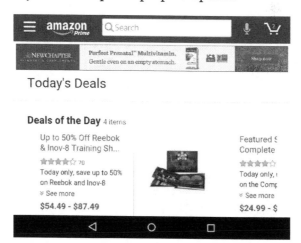

Don't Forget Amazon Prime: Your Amazon account comes with a free month of Amazon Prime (unless you've already used up this option). This opens up all kinds of free content possibilities, including the Fire ebook lending library and Prime Instant Video, plus you get free 2-day shipping on your non-digital Amazon orders.

There are special categories of Prime membership, such as student and parent, which have some restrictions on free content, so be sure to do a bit of research before you pay the fee and buy into the program.

A great feature in the Shop Amazon app is **Shop and Compare Items**. When you see a product you want to bookmark for later, press the image and drag it into the lower left corner of your screen. The shopping app will collect these items in a tray across the bottom of your screen as a new private wish list. To manage your tray selections, press and hold the item in the tray to move it to another wish list or delete it. Tap the menu icon with three vertical dots in the lower left corner to minimize or close the tray.

4. USING APPS

Applications, which we call "apps" throughout this book, are mini software programs that perform specialized tasks on your smartphone or tablet. Because they are so specific, they run lean and don't take up much room on your Fire 7's internal storage drive. There are apps for just about every task you can think of, and probably some you haven't thought of yet! Apps really are what make your Fire fun.

The operating system on your Fire 7 is based on the Android operating system, which puts thousands of Android apps at your fingertips. Not all of them - unfortunately some Android apps just won't run on the Fire - but you still have thousands to choose from, and you can download them right from the Amazon App Store to your Fire 7. The best part is that a lot of them are free! For the inside track on some of the best apps available, check out our companion book, - **250+ Best Kindle Fire HDX and HD Apps for the New Kindle Fire Owner**.

The 7 inch Fire ships with several apps pre-installed, with their icons displayed in the App Grid. They include:

• Silk web browser app

• FreeTime app

• Email, Contacts, and Calendar apps

• Weather app

• Maps app

• Calculator app

• Clock app

• Shop Amazon app

- Amazon Offers app

- Specific Amazon store apps for Kindle, music, Audible audiobooks, video, games and apps

- Goodreads app

- Fire 7 device apps for camera, documents, videos, and photos

- Firefly app

- Washington Post app

Help app and Settings app: These are simply shortcuts to the same items found in the Quick Settings Menu. (See **Chapter 2**)

Free Time: This app comes pre-installed on your Fire and lets you set up a custom selection of content for up to 4 kids. Simply follow the prompts to create separate profiles based on that child's individual preferences and assign your choice of books, apps, and videos to each profile.The Free Time app itself is free, while Free Time Unlimited is

a monthly subscription service for the app that delivers Amazon-selected children's videos, books, educational apps, movies, and television shows.

This is very smart marketing on Amazon's part - they are introducing very young users to the Fire 7 in hopes of making them users for life.

Free Time content is aimed at children ages 3 through 8 and is drawn from big-name kids' media producers like Disney, Sesame Street, Nickelodeon, and even PBS, so your kids can combine learning with entertainment.

There's also a teen profile option aimed at young people ages 11 through 17. The per-user price is quite reasonable, and with Amazon Prime, it's even better.

Firefly: What the Firefly app does is give you the ability to scan pretty much anything in the real, physical world and instantly offers up information about that thing. So in fact, whether Firefly is good for you the user will depend entirely on how and when you use it. The app is linked to the Amazon store, so the most obvious use is to scan items that you wish to purchase and check if Amazon has them in stock or offers them at a lower price. Essentially it saves you from having to type the name of the item into your device – plus Firefly can recognize barcodes and QR codes, which makes things even easier.

Another cool aspect of Firefly is that it can also recognize over 245,000 movies and TV episodes, 160 live TV channels, and 35 million songs – in mere seconds. Pretty cool if you're listening to a new tune you love but don't know who's singing it!

In fact, the range of items Firefly can recognize is astonishingly large and includes:

- Books, DVDs, Blu-ray discs, CDs, and video games

- Packaged household products

- Barcodes and QR codes

- Certain artwork

- Wine (in conjunction with the Vivino app)

- Music and songs

- Movies and TV shows

So, here is how you use the Firefly app:

First make sure your Fire tablet has an active wireless connection.

Hold your Fire in landscape orientation and swipe down from the top of the screen then tap the Firefly icon.

Next aim the rear-facing camera at the item you want to scan, or hold your tablet near the source of any audio, or up to your TV screen for video.

You will need to hold your Fire quite steady and close to the item you want to scan, and make sure there isn't any glare or shadow. For music and video, make sure that there isn't any background noise.

You will then see Firefly lights on the screen hover around and highlight the object. To identify songs, tap the Music icon, and to identify movies or TV shows, tap the Video icon.

If Firefly can identify the item, music or video, within seconds a label with an icon of the item or content will appear on the right side of the screen. Tap the label for additional information.

If Firefly can't identify the product, try scanning it again – if it's a packaged item, then scan the barcode instead. Also you can tap on the screen whilst scanning to help Firefly focus on the item. If you still have no luck then tap the label to submit feedback to Amazon.

Also good to know is that Firefly will stop by itself after a period of inactivity; just tap the screen to restart.

To exit Firefly, simply swipe down from the top of the screen to show the navigation bar on the right side of the screen, and then tap the back arrow or Home icon.

Where people find the Firefly app to be a bit intrusive is the fact that the app automatically saves scanned item results in the search history of your device.

Furthermore, Firefly images and audio are also saved in the Cloud. This means – a little annoyingly – that there are two (simple) sets of steps you have to take in order to fully delete the scanned item from your Fire.

To delete Firefly history from your device:

Swipe from the right of the Firefly window. Your most recent searches will be displayed; simply tap the Delete icon to remove it from your history.

To delete Firefly history from the Cloud:

Go to your account on the Amazon website, choose the **Manage Your Content and Devices** page, select the history you want to remove and click on the **Delete** button. You also can contact customer service to do this.

Get Your Game On

Amazon classifies its downloadable games as apps, so they appear

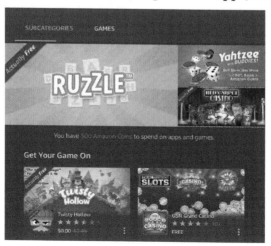

in two content categories: in the app category with all kinds of other apps, and in the games category, which displays only games. To access this library, tap **Games** in the Category Bar.

Tap **Store** to see which games Amazon is promoting on the Games page, and use the search box and on-screen keyboard to find the games of your choice. More categories of games are available when you swipe left to right to bring up the sidebar menu.

Many games have a Test Drive button that allows you check the game out for a short time before you download it. Tap the price button to purchase the game, and then tap **Download** to download it to your device. where it will appear in both the All and Downloaded libraries.

Like all other Fire apps, games must actually be stored on your device before you can use them.

Downloading Apps from Amazon

To find and download an app, go to your Fire tablet's Home screen, tap **Apps** in the Category Bar, and tap **Store**.

Amazon Underground: Under your Apps Library display in the Amazon Apps Store you'll see Recommended for You in Amazon Underground. This new Amazon program is a collection of apps for the Fire, other Amazon devices, and Android devices that are actually free, with no in-app subscriptions or extra charges for add-ons. Ironically, the downloadable Underground app for searching the collection isn't available for the Fire, or even the Fire Phone - it's only available for Android devices.

Still, your Fire's Apps content category has a good Underground search function that you can find by tapping Library and swiping left to right to open the sidebar menu. Apps that qualify for Amazon Underground all carry the Actually Free diagonal banner in the App Store.

Just keep one thing in mind: Amazon won't let you use its Underground apps until you turn on the Collect App Usage Data under **Apps & Games** in the Settings menu. Amazon turns this function on by default to keep track of how often and how long you use your downloaded apps.

The Underground store page is here: *www.lyntons.com/undergound*

Keep scrolling down in the App Store to see more Recommended for You selections based on your browsing history. Swipe from left to right to display the sidebar menu, where you'll find even more ways to search for apps. Tap the app's icon to read its description and learn more about it.

If you're anxious to get started and don't want to read more right away, you might want to start by downloading some popular free apps from the App Store. Tap the magnifying glass icon at the top of the App store window to open the search box and onscreen keyboard. You can find apps like Netflix, the Weather Channel, ESPN ScoreCenter, and more, along with a number of games. Free apps are downloaded with Amazon's standard 1-Click Ordering, but your account will show a charge of $0.00. (Remember that Netflix has "in-app purchase" meaning that it charges its own monthly subscription fee for you to use the app to stream video.)

You might notice some small print in the App Store telling you that you have some Amazon Coins to spend on apps and games. This is virtual money that Amazon manages for you so you can use it to buy... you guessed it...more apps! Amazon makes a token Coins deposit for you when you register your Fire tablet, and you can purchase more Coins by swiping left to right and choosing *Amazon Coins* from the sidebar menu.

The next step is one you shouldn't skip - use the Amazon App Store search box to find and install an Android Security App on your Fire. Check out the **Norton Mobile Security Kindle Tablet Edition** (*www.amazon.com/dp/B008R5RGAC*), which screens all new data you load to your Fire 7 for viruses and other nasties. You also might take a look at Lookout Security & Antivirus Fire Edition (*www. amazon.com/dp/B00AQ398AY*), which screens for viruses and also provides theft protection by tracing your Fire 7's Location-Based Services signal (don't use the links above if you live outside the US, instead search for them by name directly on your Fire in the app store or go to the app store at Amazon.co.uk. There are many other Android security apps with similar functions. Even though you will be downloading from Amazon, you should do your own due diligence.

When you find an app you want to download, it is a good idea to check out the developer's reputation by seeing if they provide their company name, and whether they are selling other apps besides this one. With an app that is advertised as free, make sure that it really is completely free or whether an additional fee is required (called an "in-app purchase") to use it. Make sure you understand the permissions you have to give this app to work on your Fire. It seems like overkill, and we don't always do it ourselves when downloading well-known apps, but those "freebies of the day" often come out of nowhere. So trust, but verify!

To download an app, tap the price button near the description. If the app isn't free, your 1-Click Ordering account will be charged and the button will change to Get App. Free apps actually register as a sale in your 1-Click Ordering account, but the amount shows as $0.00. Tap the *Get App* button and the app will be automatically downloaded to your Fire tablet.

When it finishes, tap the **Open** button to use it. If you don't want to use it right away, you can find it later by tapping **Apps** from the Home screen Category Bar to look for it. If you have downloaded or opened it recently, it also will appear in the Apps Grid. Note that apps must be downloaded to your Fire tablet before you can open them, unlike the other content categories on the Category Bar.

You can also buy Fire apps from your PC or Mac computer's browser and have them sent directly to your Fire. Your Amazon account will automatically detect that you have a Fire registered and will send your download directly to your device. As soon as you power up your Fire, or tap Sync Device from the Settings Menu, the app will download and open.

The Amazon App Store lists about 30 categories of apps. All these selections can be overwhelming, so we suggest that you go with a basic list at first and round out your selections later on. One good rule of thumb for downloading apps is to look at the Amazon customer reviews. Apps that average 3 stars or fewer, or have very few reviews, are probably (but not always) not as good a bet as an app with hundreds of good reviews.

Here is our favorite "must-have" list for your first visit to the Amazon App Store. Again, if you're outside the US don't use the links but search for them by name via your Fire tablet search box or at the app store at Amazon.co.uk.

Netflix (_www.amazon.com/dp/B005ZXWMUS_) - lets you watch movies and TV shows on your Fire when you order the in-app subscription or use your existing subscription information. If you're new to this service, downloading the free app gives you a one-month free trial.

Spotify (_www.amazon.com/dp/B00KLBR6IC_) - You will never run out of new music to discover when you connect to Spotify. With their free or premium service you can listen to favorite artists or albums or simply choose a playlist that suits your mood.

TuneIn (_www.amazon.com/dp/B004GYY714_) - If you like listening to the radio for talk or music then prepare yourself for TuneIn. With over 100,000 real radio stations and more than four million podcasts streaming it's safe to say there's something for everyone.

Flixster (*www.amazon.com/dp/B004HXHVZ8*) - is the "must have" app for anyone who loves movies. Stay right up to date with new film and DVD releases, read reviews via Rotten Tomatoes and find out about local show times and even book tickets.

AccuWeather (*www.amazon.com/dp/B005K17RU0*) - is the stand-out app for keeping abreast of the weather where you are. Updated every 15 minutes with an attractive interactive layout, download for free and make sure you never get caught in the rain again.

Waze Social GPS (*www.amazon.com/dp/B009ZFPQOQ*) - Driving and navigation just got social! Join drivers in your area who share real-time traffic & road info to save time, gas money, and improve daily commuting for all.

Angry Birds (*www.lyntons.com/angrybirds*) - is the most popular game app franchise in the world. Help the colorful birds heap payback on the green pigs. Be sure to download a Fire Tablet edition. The basic version is free, but there are numerous upgrades that aren't.

Drawing Pad (*www.amazon.com/dp/B004WGGQPQ*) - get creative anywhere, no matter what your level or age, if you love to draw or doodle you'll love this arty app.

Minecraft (*www.amazon.com/dp/B00992CF6W*) - If you don't know what Minecraft is...ask your children/grandchildren!

Flow Free (*www.amazon.com/dp/B008JGSM6G*) - A gentle but satisfying game, just connect the matching colors to create your free flowing pipe network. Starts off easy but soon gets tricky.

For a whole lot more great apps, both free and paid, to suit just about every conceivable need, you can also check out our companion book - **250+ Best Kindle Fire HDX and HD Apps for the New Kindle Fire Owner**.

Uninstalling Apps

If you download a lot of apps, your Fire tablet's data storage will fill up quickly. It's a good idea to do a bit of housecleaning once a month or so and get rid of any apps you aren't using. Remember that any app you order from Amazon will always be available in your Amazon Cloud library if you want to download and re-install it. Alternatively remember that you can now buy a microSD memory card and slip it into the microSD slot on the side of your Fire 7 to store your games and apps there.

To uninstall an app, tap the *Apps* content category in the Category Bar. Tap *Library* and tap *Downloaded*. Tap the menu icon with three vertical dots next to the app you want to remove and tap Delete from Device. The app is now gone from your Fire tablet but still stored safely in your Amazon Cloud library.

Once you have uninstalled an app, it won't be updated when you sync your device unless you manually re-install it. To re-install, tap *Apps* in the Navigation Bar, tap *All*, and tap the orange arrow icon to download it. Apps stored on your Fire tablet are visible in the Downloaded section of the Apps Library. Be careful **NOT to tap** Delete from Cloud and delete a paid app from your Cloud library, or you will have to buy it again to re-install it!

Force-Closing Apps

If an app stops working, the best solution is to just force-close it. Sweep down from the top of your screen to open the Quick Settings Menu. Tap **Settings**, tap **Apps & Games** and then tap **Manage All Applications** to bring up a list of the apps installed on your Fire. Tap the icon for the stuck application and tap **Force Stop** to close it.

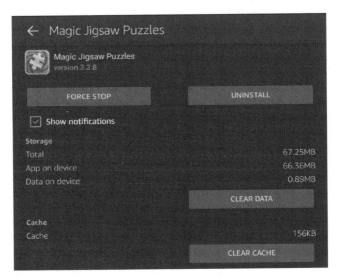

Installing Third-Party Apps

At first it may seem as if the selection of apps in the Amazon store is endless, but in reality, Amazon offers only a small percentage of the more than 500,000 apps available for Android. For a taste of what you're missing, take a look at the selection in the Google Play App Store (*play.google.com/store/apps*) and see if it seems worth your while to install apps on your Fire from outside the Amazon App Store.

This process isn't always straightforward, and some Android apps simply won't work on your Fire, but it's worthwhile if you have a bit of tech skill or you don't mind spending some time to figure it out. Note that we're not talking about "rooting," which involves installing new firmware on your Fire to enable the installation of third-party apps. Rooting will void your Fire warranty and open you up to all kinds of operating problems unless you really know what you're doing.

Amazon has built a menu item for installing third-party apps on your Fire, so it's safe to say they allow it. Tap **Settings** in the Apps Grid, then tap **Security**. Tap **Apps from Unknown Sources** and so the switch icon turns orange. This sets up your Fire tablet to install apps from sources outside of the Amazon App Store.

Be sure to download and install an Android Security App as described earlier in this chapter before you go any further. This is especially critical with online app stores, where an app can come from just about anywhere.

Some good places to find apps include the Opera App Store - (*apps. opera.com/en_us/*) - operated by the company that developed the Opera browser and SlideMe - (*www.slideme.org/*). Both of these sites feature Android apps for downloading and are high profile enough to reduce the risk of installing something buggy.

If you want to transfer apps from another device to your Fire, first go to the Amazon App Store and install the ES File Explorer app (*www. amazon.com/dp/B008K6HN8I*) on your 7 inch Fire.

This nifty app lets you manage the stored files on your Fire just as you would on your Mac or PC. Next, use the file explorer software on your desktop or laptop computer to transfer the app files you want from your Android phone or other device to your computer's hard drive.

Look for the extension .APK, which is the Android app file extension. Then transfer the app from your computer to your Fire, either with the mini USB cable, or as an attachment in an email to yourself (See **Chapter 8** for details of how to do this). Finally, use the ES File Explorer app to find and install each new app.

Non-Amazon apps don't install and open automatically like the ones you download from the Amazon App Store. There are three different methods we use to find and open Android apps on our Fire tablet.

Web Downloads: Open the Silk browser from the Apps Grid. Swipe from left to right to display the sidebar menu. Tap the Downloads button and look for your Android app, which should show an .APK extension. Tap it to install. If you get an error message, try tapping Notifications.

View Notifications: Look in the status bar across the top of your screen for a small number in a circle just to the right of your device name. If you see one, swipe the status bar down to see your notifications. If your Android app appears in the list with the .APK extension, tap it and see if the app will install.

File Exploring App: If neither of the above options work, install the ES File Explorer app as we describe above and open it. You should see several rows of blue folders. Locate the one marked Downloads and tap it to see the contents. Locate the app with the .APK extension and tap it to install.

If the installation process starts, you will need to read and accept permissions for that app and wait for the installation to complete. After that, tap *Open* at the bottom of the installation screen. If all goes well, your Android app will behave just like the Amazon apps on your Fire from now on.

We have found that the Fire gets mixed results with apps that we downloaded to our Android phone from Google Play - some of them only work partially on our Fire tablet, and some don't work at all. But it's the closest thing to putting Android functionality on your Fire that you can get without rooting, and we kind of like the challenge!

5. READING BOOKS AND NEWSSTAND ITEMS

Amazon got its start in the book selling business, and nobody does it better. It has the largest database of book titles in the world, and the bookstore is a great place to browse and do research. Amazon's development of the Fire tablet as an ebook reader was another history-making event. The technology has grown so quickly that looking at our Fire tablet today it's hard to believe that the original device was a simple e-reader with a black and white screen that could only display ebooks!

Buying Books from Amazon

To shop for ebooks on Amazon, tap **Books** in the Category Bar on your Fire's home screen and tap **Store**.

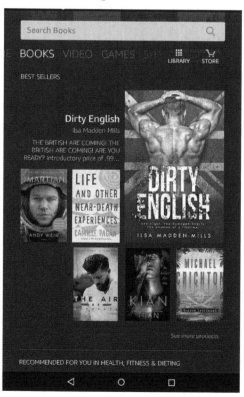

The first thing you will see in the Amazon Book Store below your Books Library is Recommended for You in Kindle Unlimited, a paid subscription program that gives you access to about 800,000 ebooks for a $9.99 monthly subscription fee. If you're interested, there's a 30-day free trial. Below that is the Recommended for You list, which Amazon carefully puts together from your previous search and buying history, and a list of Best Sellers. Additional categories are available by swiping from left to right to display the sidebar menu. You can browse the Book Store using any of these categories.

To learn more about a book, tap its cover. From the book's information page, you can read its description and see its Amazon reader reviews. Tapping the Download Sample button will download a sample excerpt to your Fire. Tap the Read Now button when the download finishes to see if it is something you want to buy.

To mark a book to look at later, tap the More Options button and tap Add to Wish List, which will store it in your Amazon Wish List. To see your Wish List, swipe from left to right to display the sidebar menu and tap Wish List to display the list.

To search for a certain book title, tap the magnifying glass icon at the top of any Book Store page to display the Search box and type the book's title, author, or keywords into it using the Fire's onscreen keyboard. You can also search the book database by its ISBN number.

To buy and download a book, tap the Buy button near the description. Amazon will charge your 1-Click Ordering account for the price of the book and the button will change to say Downloading. If you are downloading a free title, it will still register as a sale in your 1-Click Ordering account in the amount of $0.00. When the download is complete, the button will change again to say Read Now. Amazon gives you the option of canceling your order if you bought the book by mistake.

You can also buy Kindle ebooks from your PC or Mac computer and send them directly to your Fire. Your Amazon account will automatically know that you have a Fire registered and will list your device in the drop-down menu marked "Deliver to" on the right side of your browser screen under the Buy button. Select your Fire from the list, and as soon as you power up your Fire, or tap *Sync Device* from the Settings Menu, the book will download and open.

Reading Books on Your Fire 7

Any new, unopened books on your Fire tablet will appear in your Books Library with a strip across the cover that says New. You can find your newly purchased books by tapping *Books* from the Home screen Category Bar. If you are in the process of reading a book, the cover will display the percentage of the book you have finished so far. Double tap the cover icon that appears in your Library to open the book and read it, or tap it once and wait for it to open automatically. Turn the pages by swiping in the direction you want to move, or tapping the side of the screen.

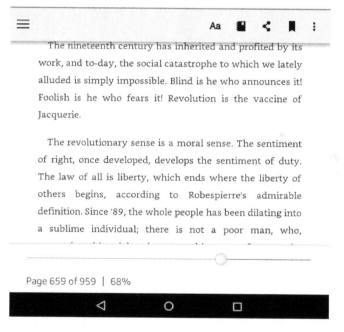

When you open a book to read, the Fire defaults to full screen mode and hides all navigation icons, which can leave you feeling stranded until you learn how to escape. Simply tap once anywhere on the book page, or swipe from the top or bottom of the screen. The NavigationBar with the Home and Back icons will appear at the bottom, and the Reading Toolbar will appear at the top. You will also see a slider showing how much of the book you've finished.

You can use the slider as a Go To command to move to a numbered location within the book. If you swipe left to right while these menus are visible, you'll bring up a full table of contents that you can tap to go to the beginning of each chapter. Tap the page again to hide these menus.

Word Runner: Some readers find this feature really speeds up their reading by displaying words one at a time in large print at a pace present to their individual reading style.

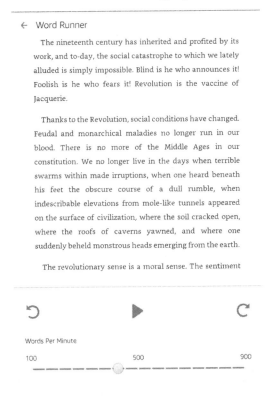

To enable it, tap the menu icon with three vertical dots on the Reading Toolbar, tap **Word Runner**, and tap the forward arrow to play. Drag the speed bar to adjust the display speed. If you tap and hold the screen, it will activate the Brake so you can catch up.

Managing Your Book Library: Books can really fill up your Fire's data storage, so Amazon gives you two tabs at the top of your Book Library screen. Titles displayed in the All tab are your complete collection of book purchases stored in your Amazon Cloud library, while the titles shown in the Downloaded tab are the ones you have downloaded from your Amazon Cloud library to your Fire device.

If you want to read a book from the cloud that you haven't stored on your device, then you can only access it when your Fire is connected to a wireless network. This leaves more data storage space open on your Fire, but remember that you can't access the cloud while reading at the beach. If you plan to travel to a location with no wireless access and want to read on your Fire, do a bit of advance planning and download the books you want to read so they are stored on your device.

To download or remove a book from your Fire, tap **Books** in the Category Bar and tap **Library**. To download a book from your Amazon Cloud library, tap **All**, and tap the book's cover to download it. To remove a book from your device, tap Downloaded, and press and hold on the cover until a trash can icon appears in the upper right corner of your screen. Tapping the trash can icon takes the book off your Fire tablet but leaves it in your Amazon Cloud library to download again at any time. Don't delete any books from your library in the cloud, or you will have to buy them again to download them.

Fire 7 Reading Accessibility Features

The Fire tablet ebook reader app lets you customize your reading experience from the Reading Toolbar. To display the toolbar, tap the screen while displaying any book in the reader. From here adjust the appearance of the reader screen via the options across the top. Tap *Aa* to customize the reader's background and text colors, enlarge or reduce the text size, change the display font, and even change the spacing. If you tap the menu icon with the three vertical dots and choose *Additional Settings*, there are also some other very interesting options and functions here to choose from which can greatly improve your user experience.

These include:

Text-to-Speech: For those books that are Text-to-Speech enabled, this button will let your Fire read text to you! To access it, tap the menu icon with three vertical dots on the Reading Toolbar, tap *Additional Settings* at the bottom, and tap *Text-to-Speech* to turn it on for books that are enabled for this feature.

X-Ray: This is a great tool for reading club fans and students. In books that are X-Ray enabled, you can use this option to find passages in a book that mention the same concept, character, places and other useful information about the book or the author. To access it, tap the menu icon with three vertical dots on the Reading Toolbar, and tap X-Ray button in the menu to bring up the full range of these passages for you to explore.

Share: The Share option on the Reading Toolbar is a super quick way for you to copy and share sections of a book via Twitter or Facebook.

Bookmark: Simply tap the upper right corner of the book page to create a bookmark on the page you're currently reading. Fire will automatically go to this page when you next open that book. To display your bookmarks, tap anywhere on the book page to bring up the Reading Toolbar and tap the *Bookmarks icon* on the right.

Making notes and highlighting text: Tap the screen on the first word of a section you want to highlight, then drag your finger along the section. Lift your finger and an option box will pop up asking you what you want to do with the section (either add a note, highlight or share). You can access your notes and highlights via the Notes option on the Reading Toolbar. You can also see sections of a book that other readers have highlighted by turning on the Popular Highlights option. Swipe downward from the top edge to display the Quick Settings Menu, tap *Settings*, and tap *Apps & Games*. Tap the *Amazon Application Settings* sub menu, tap *Reader Settings*, and tap P*opular Highlights* to turn it on or off.

Word Wise: When activated, this feature shows brief inline hints for unknown words in a book. You can set the word difficulty level that triggers the hint, making it ideal for young people learning to read. Tap the menu icon with the three vertical dots and tap *Word Wise* to set it up or turn it off.

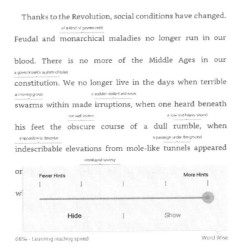

Dictionary: The reader app also features a built-in dictionary. Tap and hold any word to bring up a quick definition. If you click *Full Definition*, the dictionary will expand to show you the complete entry within the dictionary. The dictionary lets you search the book for the word, search on Wikipedia, or search the web for it. You can also translate the word by typing your own language into the translate box in the corner of the definition box and selecting the language you want to translate it into - neat!

Goodreads: Amazon created yet more buzz in the book industry when it acquired Goodreads and its 20 million members. The Fire lets Goodreads members sync their Fire 7 and Goodreads accounts to automatically post their Amazon book purchases to Goodreads. This feature allows sharing of "Want to Read" lists and rapid exchange of reading lists between Goodreads friends. To access Goodreads, tap Books in the Category Bar, tap Library, and tap the Goodreads button at the top of your library screen, or swipe left to right to display the sidebar menu and tap Goodreads. You will need your Goodreads login and password information to access your account.

MatchBook: Amazon has rolled out its MatchBook feature, which offers customers a discount price on the ebook edition of any book title they initially purchased in print. Go to *www.amazon.com/ kindlematchbook* to see a list of eligible titles and a list of books you've purchased that are available in MatchBook. More titles are being added to this program all the time, so if you don't see the book you want on the list, check it again from time to time.

Downloading Free Ebooks

The Fire 7 has made books more affordable than ever, and free titles are easy to find, both in the Amazon Book Store and on third-party websites. Here are some places to look for free reading material.

Amazon has two special programs that offer free books. The first is Kindle Select, which allows publishers to make their books free to build readership. You can browse the top 25 Select titles of the week by swiping left to right in the Books Library to display the sidebar menu and tapping **Kindle Select 25**. Another way to browse the Select program is from a third-party website that collects free titles. These tend to come and go on the web, but a quick Google search from the Silk browser on "free Amazon ebooks" will bring up several sites that list books in the Select program.

The second Amazon free books program is Free Popular Classics. These are older titles in the public domain whose copyright has expired. Thousands of classic works of literature are available for download to your Fire tablet, including Les Misérables, A Tale of Two Cities, Alice in Wonderland, and Jane Eyre. To browse this collection, type free popular classics into the search box.

Internet Archive: This nonprofit site has collected over 2.5 million book titles that you can read on your Fire, but you will need to download each ebook to your Mac or PC first. In your computer's browser, go to **archive.org** and search for a title, or scroll down to browse the subcollections. Choose a book, click **Details**, and look in the right sidebar for the Kindle version download link. Save the file to your computer. From your hard drive, you can transfer the file to your Fire using either the micro USB cable, or by emailing it to yourself as an attachment and downloading the book in your Fire's email app. See **Chapter 8** for more file transfer options.

Open Library: This enormous free library contains 1 million free ebook titles, but not all of them are available for the Fire tablet, and some of them require you to register first. From your Mac or PC browser window, go to **openlibrary.org** and click the "1,000,000 free ebook titles" link near the top of the screen. Search for the title you want, or browse by subject, author, or keyword from the menu at the top left. Make sure you check the box that says "Show Only Ebooks" before you run each search. Click on a title to see whether you can download it as a MOBI file, or if there's a Send to Kindle Option. If you can, click it to download and transfer it from your hard drive to your Fire as we explain above. For some titles, you can also download a Fire edition directly to your device from the Silk browser.

Project Gutenburg: This free site holds 50,000 titles. Use your Mac or PC to browse to gutenberg.org and search for the title you want, or browse by category. When you find a book, click the Kindle with Images link and download it to your hard drive, then transfer it over to your Fire 7 using one of the methods explained above.

ManyBooks: This library has 33,000 free ebooks but you have to sign up for a free subscription with your email address. Use your computer to search for a title or browse the categories, then click on a title and use the Download menu on the right to grab the MOBI version so you can transfer it over to your Fire tablet.

Borrowing Books from Amazon

Amazon is more than a bookstore - it also functions as a gigantic lending library. If you have an Amazon Prime membership, then you can borrow books for free, which really is an incredible deal. Without Prime, you will pay a fee to borrow a book. The Lending Library program limits you to one borrow per month, but there are no due dates. Only Kindle e-reader, Fire tablet, and Fire Phone owners are eligible for this program.

To borrow a book on your Fire, tap **Books** in the Category Bar and tap **Store**. Swipe left to right to display the sidebar menu and tap **Kindle Owners Lending Library** to bring up a list of titles you can borrow for free with Prime. Tap any title to display the book's information page, and tap Borrow for Free. The book will download to your Fire and open for you to read. You can add notes and highlights to a borrowed book just as you can for a book you own, and they will be saved in your account.

The easiest way to return a book is simply to borrow another one. During the borrowing process, you will be prompted to return the old one. Another method is to go to the Amazon home page in the Silk browser and choose Manage Your Fire from the drop-down menu under Your Account. Tap the Actions button next to the title you want to return and follow the prompts. You can also follow the same process on your PC or Mac.

Borrowing Amazon Books Through Your Local Library: Amazon's Overdrive program allows more than 10,000 libraries in the United States to lend Fire titles to their patrons who have Amazon accounts - no Prime membership required! Each library has its own lending policy, but generally there are restrictions on how many ebooks you can borrow at a time, and how long you can check them out. You will also need to set up an account and PIN for the library you are using.

From your Fire's Silk browser or your laptop or desktop computer, use your library's online card catalog to search for ebooks (some libraries call them digital books). Click on the title and click "Get Ebook" or a similar-sounding link. At this point you will need to select your library name and type in your PIN number. The book and its description will appear in a new screen. Click the Borrow button and choose Kindle format from the drop-down menu. Overdrive will now take you to the Amazon website. Click the Get Library Book button on the right and download it to your Fire or your computer. If you used your computer for this, you will need to transfer the book's MOBI file to your Fire using the instructions above or in Chapter 8.

If the Borrow button has been replaced with a Place a Hold button, then you will have to place a hold on the title to read it later - Amazon Overdrive limits the number of copies of any single title that can be checked out in your library system at one time. Unfortunately, if your title is checked out, you will have to backtrack several screens to search for another one, and possibly enter your PIN again.

The advice above is one way to go. Another option is to download and use the Overdrive Media Console (*www.amazon.com/dp/ B00850NK6I*) app which you can download for free from the Amazon app store (use the link or just search for "Overdrive"). Using this app should allow you to do everything necessary to complete the whole process from one place. We haven't used this app and have heard mixed feedback with some Fire users absolutely loving it and other saying that they can't get it to work. Looking at recent reviews suggests that improvement and fixes have been made.

Lending Your Fire Books to a Friend: You can lend items from your Fire Book Library to one person for up to 14 days. The borrower can read it on a Kindle or Fire device, or on a PC or Mac after downloading and installing the Kindle Reader software.

To lend a book, go to the Amazon home page in the Fire Silk browser or your computer browser, and choose Manage Your Content and Devices from the drop-down menu under Your Account. Tap the Actions button next to the title you want to lend and choose Lend This Book.

Amazon will prompt you for the borrower's password. Click the Send Now button. Note that lending is not available for some Amazon titles, and that each of your books can only be loaned once. You will not be able to read the book while it is out on loan.

Buying and Reading Newsstand Items

The Fire Newsstand is where you can subscribe to magazines, newspapers, and blogs that require a subscription fee. Tap **Newsstand** in the Category Bar and tap **Store**. Under your Newsstand Library items you will see a display of Recommended for You magazine titles and some best sellers.

To start a subscription through 1-Click Ordering, tap any item and tap the Subscribe Now button or Try Free for 30 days. Newsstand items with interactive features will require a free app for that item, which you can download from the App Store and then activate your subscription with an in-app purchase.

To view your Newsstand items, tap **Newsstand** in the Category Bar and tap **Library**. Fire only keeps the current issue of each Newsstand

item on your device. To see up to 12 back issues of any magazine or 14 back issues of any newspaper, tap the title in the All tab of your Library and tap the back issue you want to download to your Fire.

Older back issues can be downloaded from your Subscription Settings page. You can access this page a couple of different ways. The easiest way is to swipe down from the top to open the Quick Settings menu, tap Settings, tap My Account, tap My Account Settings, a Settings, and tap Subscriptions. Sign in and use the Actions button to deliver past issues to your Fire tablet. If you have purchased a Newsstand item with a free 30-day trial, you can cancel your subscription from this page before Amazon charges your credit card for it.

You can also use the Silk browser or your computer browser to navigate from Amazon's home page to your Amazon account page and finally to your *Manage Your Content and Devices* page. Choose your device from the *Devices tab*. Using the Manage menu on the left, you can download back issues and activate or cancel subscriptions to newsstand items using the Actions button on the right.

6. LISTENING TO MUSIC

Your Fire tablet makes a great music player. We were surprised to find that holding the Fire tablet doesn't interfere with the sound quality, nor does a properly designed protective case made specifically for the Fire (see **Chapter 10**). You can make your Fire sound even better with a good pair of headphones (see **Chapter 10**).

Buying Music from Amazon

To shop for music on Amazon, tap *Music* in the Category Bar on your Fire's home screen and tap *Store*. Their inventory is running at over 30 million songs, so there's something there for everyone.

The Amazon Music Store displays lots of eye-catching photos and graphics to entice you into expanding your listening library. Tap the *Store* icon to see several rows of recommendations customized for you based on your previous purchase and listening history. To see additional categories, tap one of the tabs at the top of the Store screen to browse by Genres, Best Sellers, or New Releases. You can browse the Music Store using any of these categories. Tap any thumbnail to learn more about the selection. From the selection's information page, you can tap the circled number next to any track to listen to a sample clip.

To search for an album or song, tap the *Search box* and type an album, song, or artist into it using the Fire tablet's onscreen keyboard.

To buy a selection, tap the *price* button, which will change to say *Buy Now*. Tapping it again will charge your 1-Click Ordering account for the price of the selection and store it in your Amazon Cloud library. Free music still registers as a sale in your 1-Click Ordering account in the amount of $0.00. A pop-up menu will open and give you the choice of either going to your Music library and listening to your purchase, or continuing to shop.

Prime Music: Amazon has sweetened the deal for its Prime members by offering them a huge catalog of 1 million songs, as well as albums, pre-selected Prime Playlists, and stations, absolutely free. You can also create your own playlists by mixing up Prime Music selections with your own musical tracks and saving the result.

If you're a Prime member, you can browse for Prime Music selections in the Amazon Music Store by tapping *Music* in the Category Bar. Tap *Library* or *Store* and swipe left to right to display the sidebar menu. Tap *Prime Music* and scroll down your Fire touchscreen to see Amazon's selection of free songs in the Prime Music catalog.

To see additional categories, tap one of the tabs at the top of the Store screen to browse by Stations, Playlists, Songs, or Genres. Just tap the + *icon* to add a Prime Music song to your Amazon Cloud library for free. To add a song from a Playlist to your library, tap the *Add* button next to it, or add the entire playlist by tapping the menu icon with the three vertical dots next to the playlist and tap *Add to Library* from the pop-up menu.

You can also use the Search box on any page in your Music Library to hunt for your favorite song, artist, album, or genre using the keyboard. To narrow down your search, tap *All Genres* in the top left corner and choose your favorite type of music to browse through. You can also pick out Prime Music selections while browsing the full music library by looking for a selection with the diagonal Prime banner across its icon.

Any Prime Music selections you add to your Music Library display right along with your other songs and albums, no matter how you sort the items (by album, song, artist, or genre). The Prime Playlists section under "Your Playlists" shows the Prime Playlists you've added to your library.

Prime members can listen to their Prime Music selections in their Amazon Cloud library in the cloud on virtually any device they own, as well as directly on Amazon.com. Prime Music can only be downloaded to phones and tablets that support Amazon Music. This app is built into your Fire, but you must download it to other devices, and your Prime Music selections can't be exported to other devices. You must access your downloaded selections while connected to a wireless network every 30 days or they are automatically deleted.

Be aware that Prime Music titles come and go, so if Amazon decides to remove a selection from Prime, you will need to purchase it before you can listen to it again.

AutoRip: Like many music lovers, we still buy music CDs from Amazon. We like the album art and liner notes, and their sound quality is better than MP3 files, but of course you can't play them on a tablet or smartphone without ripping them to MP3 format first. That why we love Amazon's AutoRip service. As soon as your CD order ships, AutoRip automatically puts an MP3 copy into your Amazon Music Library, where you can listen to it from the *Cloud tab*, or download it to your Fire and play it from the *Device tab*. Not only that, it automatically adds all of your Amazon CD purchases dating back to 1998 to your Music Library - awesome! There's only one catch: some of your CDs might not be eligible for this service, depending on their copyright terms - boo!

Listening to Music

To listen to music on your Fire, tap *Music* from the Home screen Category Bar and tap *Library* to scroll through your collection to find an album, song or playlist. Swipe left to right to display the sidebar menu, where you can view your recent activity in your Music library or scroll through your entire library. Tap the *Library icon* to see the music stored online in Amazon Cloud, or tap *Offline Library* to view the music stored on your Fire 7. You can also tap *Settings* in the sidebar menu to change how your device handles music storage and downloads.

Tap any thumbnail to open and play a selection. You can also select a playlist by tapping its name. (We explain how to create playlists later in this chapter.) When you play a song from an album or playlist, your Fire will move to the next song when the first one finishes. The player controls will display whenever a song is playing. Tap on the appropriate button to pause, skip to the next or previous song, shuffle, or repeat. You can use the slider here to adjust volume, or use the manual volume controls located on the side of your Fire tablet.

Amazon has rolled out a song lyrics feature for selected songs in its Music store. As you play one of these songs on your Fire, you will see the lyrics displayed on your screen and scroll line by line as the song progresses. Photos and facts about the artist are featured along with song lyrics. More and more songs are becoming available with this feature.

Listening from your Amazon Cloud Library: Your Fire contains a built-in media player for streaming music through your Fire from your Amazon Cloud library account. (See end of **Chapter 1** for more about the cloud.) Your Fire's internal data storage isn't big enough to hold an extensive music library, but your Music Library in the cloud contains your complete collection of Amazon music purchases, plus you can buy additional storage space in your Amazon Cloud Library account to add music you didn't purchase from Amazon to your Music Library.

We have found that it's more convenient to store our music in the cloud and stream it, even though it uses somewhat more battery life. To stream music stored in your Music Library, tap **Music** from the Home screen Category Bar and tap the **Library icon**. If you can only see the songs stored on your device, swipe left to right and tap **Offline Library** in the sidebar to go back to your Amazon Cloud library selections. Tap the icon for any selection to start listening.

Listening Offline: If you are traveling to a location with no Wi-Fi access, then storing as much music as you can fit on your device will be a better option. In your Music Library, swipe left to right and tap **Offline Library** in the sidebar so the switch icon turns orange. This will disable your Cloud library menu and display only the music stored on your device, where you can tap the icon of any the selection you want to listen to.

To download music from the cloud, open your Music Library from the Category Bar, tap **Library**, and make sure your Cloud Library is enabled in the sidebar menu. Find your selection on the list, tap the menu icon with the three vertical dots, and tap **Download** from the pop-up menu.. To remove a selection from your Fire, tap **Remove from Device** from the same pop-up menu. This takes the item off your Fire but leaves it in your cloud Music Library to download again at any time. Remember, don't delete any purchased music from your Amazon Cloud library, or you will have to buy it again to listen to it!

Managing Your Music Library

Creating Playlists: You can create your own playlists in your Amazon Cloud music library by adding the songs and albums you've stored in the cloud or on your Fire tablet. Tap the menu icon with the three vertical dots next to any selection and tap **Add to Playlist** in the pop-up menu. Add it to an existing playlist by tapping that list, or tap the + **symbol** labeled **Create New Playlist**. Give it a name and tap **Save** to add your selection to the new list.

To delete an item from a playlist, tap the **Library icon** and tap **Playlists** on the far left of the top menu bar. Choose the playlist you want to delete the selection from and tap the menu icon next to that selection. Tap **Remove from Playlist** in the pop-up menu to delete the item.

Prime Playlists: If you're an Amazon Prime member, check out the selection of pre-populated playlists available in for free. From the Category Bar on the Home screen tap **Music** and tap **Library**. Tap **Playlists** to bring up compilations like "Pop to Make You Feel Better" and "Singing in the Shower," as well as more conventional classic rock and techno lists. Lengths vary from 90 minutes to over 3 hours so you can tap a list and forget about it while it plays.

Transferring Your Music to Amazon Cloud Drive

All Amazon customers get unlimited free space in their Amazon Cloud library account for their Amazon content purchases. Prime members also get unlimited free storage for photos, along with 5GB for videos and document files, and space for 250MB of non-Amazon music files. Amazon Non-Prime members pay $11.99 per month for the same services after the 3 month free trial period is $59.99 per year, regardless of whether you're a Prime member

To import your personal music collection to Amazon Music, go to your music library at _www.amazon.com/musiclibrary_ from a web browser on the computer you want to import your music from. Scroll down the sidebar, click **Upload Your Music** and follow the prompts to install the Amazon Music app for your computer. The app searches your iTunes and Windows Media Player libraries, or you may manually choose the folders where your personal music collection is stored. Choose which songs to upload, or click **Upload All**.

The Amazon Music app will read most music file formats, but you will have to copy your CDs to your computer's hard drive before you can upload them. Third-party music ripper software makes this quick and easy. It's best to set the output format to MP3 to save time and to free up space on your computer's hard drive.

Buying and Listening to Audiobooks

Audiobooks have their own library that you can access from the Category Bar on the Home screen of your Fire tablet. Tap Store to shop for audiobooks on Amazon. Shopping for and managing this library is very similar to buying and managing ebooks in your Books Library (see **Chapter 5**). The Audiobooks shopping menu has a Wish List option, and it downloads your purchases automatically through your 1-Click Shopping account.

Titles you purchase are added to the your Audiobooks library, where you can call up a list of your titles by tapping *Library*. Tap *All* to display your audiobooks stored in your Amazon Cloud library, or tap *Downloaded* to display titles stored on your device. keep in mind that audiobooks take up a lot of storage space on your device. To shop by category, tap *Store* from the Audiobooks content category, swipe left to right to display the sidebar menu, and tap *Browse Categories*.

The Fire's built-in audiobook player displays a control panel where you can adjust its reading speed to slower or faster than normal, add bookmarks, pause the audio, back up 30 seconds, and adjust the playback volume. The player control panel also has a Sleep function that we really love. You can actually set your Fire to read you to sleep at night for 15 to 60 minutes, or to the end of a chapter - lovely!

You can add a note when you place a bookmark by tapping and holding the *Bookmark key* until the onscreen keyboard pops up. To display your list of bookmarks, tap the small notebook icon in the upper right corner while the audiobook is open in the player. Tap and hold any bookmark to edit your notes or delete the bookmark. Swiping left to right will display the sidebar menu with lots of options for managing your audiobook library and player. The sidebar menu also contains options for jumping from chapter to chapter and details about each audiobook title.

Although Amazon audiobooks aren't part of the Lending Library program for Prime members, we found that our local library loans out selected audiobook titles through Amazon's Overdrive program (see **Chapter 5**).

Audible: If you go to _Audible.com_ and sign up for a 30-day trial, you get a free audiobook to add to your library before the monthly subscription fee kicks in. There's also an Audible app for Android that's free to download from the Amazon App Store and offers some great features if you opt for the monthly subscription plan as an in-app purchase. Audible is an Amazon company, so their website sells the entire library of Amazon ebooks and audiobooks for you to read or listen to on your Fire tablet.

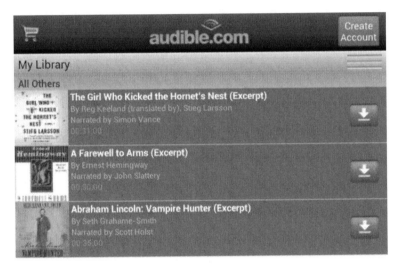

You can purchase your Audible subscription from the Amazon App store or from your Mac or PC. The cheapest plan gives you one free audiobook per month plus discounts on additional audiobook purchases, while the expanded plans cost more but give you more free audiobook downloads. We listen to a lot of audiobooks, and they aren't cheap to purchase, so this subscription plan has been worthwhile for us, and with 180,000 audiobooks to choose from, we haven't run out of material yet.

Check out Audible's Immersion Reading feature, which highlights each word of your audiobook in the text version as the word is spoken. Audible also manages Amazon's Whispersync function, which saves the highlights and bookmarks you place in your Fire ebook library and syncs them across all of your devices.

And you can also set the Audible app to be Button-Free - opening your user experience to a more fluid interaction with the use of some neat shortcuts. For example, once your book is playing through the Audible app, you need only tap anywhere on the Fire 7 screen to pause or play, swipe left or right to go backwards and forwards, swipe down to skip a chapter, and tap and hold the screen to create a bookmark.

7. WATCHING MOVIES

With its resolution display and excellent audio quality, the 7 inch Fire might be the ultimate portable video player. Amazon's video store has over 150,000 titles, and the Fire's portable size lets you take your movie watching anywhere you go. However, for the time being, Amazon's Instant Video Service is only available in the United States.

Amazon has also developed its exclusive Advance Streaming and Prediction (ASAP) technology to address a common customer complaint about internet video streaming: buffering. You've probably experienced stuttering, "hanging," and audio out of sync with the video when you play videos through your computer's web browser, and possibly with other digital media players you've tried out.

Buffering occurs because most people's broadband service isn't up to the heavy bandwidth usage demands of digital media streaming. Amazon's solution is to tap into your user history and use it to predict which movies and TV episodes you might want to watch. These titles are preloaded into your account on their server. If you buy or rent one of these titles, they're already buffered for you and waiting for instant playback – A-S-A-P.

Buying or Renting Videos from Amazon

To shop in the Amazon Instant Video store, tap *Video* in the Category Bar on your Fire's home screen. If you've already watched a selection, it will appear across the top row. Tap *Store* to go video shopping.

The top half of the store is devoted to Amazon's Prime Instant Video service. All of the videos in this category are also available without a Prime membership - they just cost more! The lower half of your screen displays Amazon's suggested videos for you based on your viewing history, Prime Original content created by Amazon, and recently added selections.

To search for a video, tap the *Search box* at the top of the Video Store page. Type a title or set of keywords using the onscreen keyboard. To delete your video search history, tap *Library* or *Store* and swipe left to right to display the sidebar menu. Select *Settings*, and then tap *Clear Video Search History*.

To use the X-Ray feature to learn more about a video, tap its thumbnail in the Video Store to see a rich selection of facts and trivia from the Internet Movie Database (IMDb), which is also available for free as an app in the Amazon App Store.

Most Video Store movies will have a *Watch Trailer* button under the thumbnail so you can see the preview. TV shows will list which seasons are available and their prices.

Swipe from left to right to display the sidebar menu, where you will find your Watch List. You can add videos you have purchased and videos you want to save for possible purchase later to this list. To scroll through the Watch List, swipe down the display of thumbnails. To mark a video in the Store to return to later, tap the **Add to Watchlist** button for that item.

For each video in the store, the Buy and Rent Buttons appear on the right side of your screen with a price shown for each. If no Rent button appears, then the video is not available for rental. Clicking one of these buttons will charge your 1-Click Ordering account so you can get the video. You can choose to start watching it right away, or save it in your Video Library.

Renting Videos: If you tap the **Rent** button, 1-Click Ordering immediately charges you for the rental. The rental period for videos is only 24 hours, but it doesn't begin until you actually start to watch the video. Be sure to select whether you want to rent the or SD version during the rental process. There is no need to return a rental video - it simply becomes unavailable when you tap it in your Video Library until you rent it again or buy it. We think that this alone is a good reason to rent your videos on Amazon!

Amazon Prime Instant Video: Thousands of videos in the Amazon store are available to Prime members for free - yes, you read that right! All Prime Instant freebies can be streamed to your Fire through your Wi-Fi connection, and Amazon now offers over half of this collection for downloading as well. This really is an incredible deal and is just one more excellent reason to buy a Prime membership.

Watching Videos

By default, all of your purchases from the Amazon Video Store are streamed to you via your Wi-Fi connection to save data storage space on your Fire tablet. Streaming requires you to be in an area with an active Wi-Fi connection, and remember that it uses up some battery juice on your device. To watch a video, tap the item in your Video Library or in your Watchlist in the sidebar menu and then tap **Watch Now**. To go back to a video you haven't finished, tap its thumbnail in your Video Library screen.

Video Player Controls: To display the video player control panel, simply tap the screen while you are watching a video. The slider allows you to turn the volume up or down. The pause button lets you pause or resume the video when you tap it. There is also a 10-second skipback button to rewind the video 10 seconds. Finally, the video scrub bar lets you move forward or backward in slow motion through the video to a frame of your choice by dragging your finger across the bar.

Watching Downloaded Videos: If you want to watch a video in a location with no Wi-Fi connection, then you will need to download it to your Fire tablet first. Tap the video's thumbnail in your Video Library or the Watch List and tap *Download* to save the video to your Fire. The menu will give you the choice of downloading the video in HD or SD format, and your answer will depend on how much storage space is left on your device and how important HD resolution is to you for this particular video.

If you want to pause or cancel the download, tap the *Download Options* button and tap *Cancel Download*. To view the downloaded video from your Fire without a Wi-Fi connection, tap the video's thumbnail and then tap *Watch Now*. Remember that some Prime Instant Video selections are not available for download.

If you want to find out more about Amazon Prime our other book **Amazon Prime & Kindle Unlimited: Newbie to Expert in 1 Hour!** - *www.amazon.com/gp/product/B00WZY5DVK* - has more info

Streaming from Third-Party Sites

Third-party video streaming services like Netflix and Hulu Plus are battling it out with Amazon for the biggest share of the video market. For the moment, Amazon seems to be winning, but if you want to try out these services, you should start by downloading their free apps from the Amazon App Store (see **Chapter 4**). Both services charge a monthly subscription fee as an in-app purchase.

Free video streaming sites such as YouTube and Vimeo have one issue with the Fire, and that is the Silk browser's lack of support for Flash video. Both of these video sharing sites are moving toward HTML5 as they phase out Flash, so this situation should continue to improve.

Watch Movies on Your TV

The Fire 7 offers two ways to watch Amazon Instant Video on your HDTV.

Second Screen: Amazon's Second Screen feature lets you stream any Amazon Instant Video through your wi-fi network from your Fire to your Amazon Fire TV, PlayStation 3 or PlayStation 4. You can fling movies and TV shows from your tablet to a big screen while using your Fire tablet as a remote to control playback and other functions. You can even browse the web, check your email, or use Amazon's X-Ray feature to learn more about the movie you're watching. To activate Second Screen, tap its icon 📲 from the movie player menu.

Display Mirroring: The Fire has a Display Mirroring selection in its Settings menu. It allows you to mirror your Fire display to compatible TV's and other media streaming devices, or an HDMI dongle such as the Fire TV Stick or Google Chromecast. This is a great way to watch Amazon Instant Video or view your photos albums.

To mirror your Fire screen, turn on your display device and make sure it's turned on and discoverable "Discoverable" means that your Fire tablet can identify and connect to the display wirelessly. Refer to the user guide that came with the display device if necessary. On your Fire, swipe down from the top and tap *Settings*, then tap *Display*, then tap *Display Mirroring*. Choose your display device and tap *Connect*. The Fire 7 will also do screen mirroring wirelessly with an HDMI dongle like the Fire TV Stick or Google Chromecast.

Coming Soon

A future Fire update will introduce a new feature called On Deck. The tablet will automatically download popular movies and TV shows while you're not using the device and hold them for you. When you're stuck without a Wi-Fi connection, that content will be waiting for you to view from your Fire.

8. WORKING WITH PHOTOS AND DOCUMENTS

With its front-facing and rear-facing cameras, the Fire tablet has joined the ranks of bona fide tablets such as the far more expensive Apple and Samsung products. You can take photos, videos, and self-portraits, and the built-in microphone makes Skype calls and video chat a reality.

Taking Photos with the Fire 7

To use the Fire 7 built-in cameras, tap the **Camera app** in the in the Apps Grid. When the app opens, tap the double arrow icon to toggle back and forth between the two cameras on your tablet. The front-facing camera faces toward you, while the rear-facing camera faces away from you.

To take a photo, tap the shutter icon ⬡. Your image will be automatically saved, but Film Strip ▣ displays recent photos in a strip across the lower edge of your screen. Tap the **Film Strip icon** to toggle between displaying and hiding the Film Strip. To delete a photo from your Fire, tap the image in the Film Strip or on the touchscreen display and tap **Delete**. Check the box labeled **Also Delete from your Cloud Drive** to completely erase the image.

To display the Camera Settings while the Camera app is open, tap the gear icon ⚙ in the upper right corner of the screen and use the toggle sliders to activate or deactivate the app's features. This menu allows you to activate or deactivate HDR (High Dynamic Range) for the rear-facing camera only, which will give you better photo quality in low light or shadowy settings.

You can also activate the Image Review feature which temporarily displays each photo you take so you can decide whether to keep or delete it. The Settings Menu also controls video quality, panorama, lenticular (rapid-fire camera shots), and **Best Shot.** This feature takes a picture just before and just after each picture you take. After you take the picture, tap the Best Shot icon in Image Review and tap the photo you want to save. To hide the Settings menu, sweep it upward.

To exit the Camera app and return to your Photo Library screen, tap the back arrow in the Navigation Bar (you might need to sweep upward from the bottom if the camera is in full screen mode). The Share icon in the Camera Roll lets you share the image via email, a Bluetooth device, Facebook, or Twitter. The pencil icon offers some nice editing features for retouching and optimizing your photos right on your Fire 7.

To enable storing your photos in your Amazon Cloud Library, activate Auto-Save from the settings menu. Swipe left to right in Camera Roll mode, scroll down and tap **Settings**, and turn Auto-Save on or off. This Settings screen is the same display you see when you tap the **gear icon** in the Camera app. It also shows your total Cloud Drive usage. If you tap **Manage Cloud Drive Storage**, the Fire will open the Amazon Cloud Drive login screen. Note that photos taken with your Fire tablet don't count against your storage limit in your Cloud Library.

Taking Videos: The rear-facing camera records videos with sound. Open the Camera app and tap the red video icon 🔴 to start recording. You can zoom in and out by pinching the screen with two fingers, or by using the volume buttons on the edge of your tablet's case. Tap the **video icon** again to stop recording and store or delete the video.

Taking Panoramic Photos: The rear-facing camera takes long photos in either a horizontal or vertical direction. Activate the Camera app from the App Grid. Open the Camera app and tap the gear icon ⚙ , then tap **Panorama**. Tap the blue capture icon and move your Fire tablet slowly in the direction you would like to capture the panoramic photo, or touch and slide the arrow in the preview strip. Tap the white square inside the blue capture icon to save.

Using Skype with the Fire 7

Skype is a free app that lets you chat with other Skype users all over the world for free with video chat, voice chat, and instant messaging. With its front-facing camera and built-in microphone, the Fire 7 is a good friend when you want to Skype.

To install the Skype app on your Fire 7, tap **Apps** from the Navigation Bar and use the search box to find it in the Amazon App Store. Download it and open it. If you're already a Skype user, log in with your user name and password, or register an account if you're a newcomer to Skype.

Before you start chatting, set up your profile by tapping the head and shoulders icon in the upper right corner of the Skype home page. From this menu you can upload a profile photo or avatar by tapping the larger head and shoulders icon that pops up. **Choose from gallery** lets you upload any photo from your Fire Photo Library, while **Take photo** activates the tablet's Camera app so you can take a self-portrait and upload it. The profile menu also lets you choose whether to let your contacts know you're available, or keep your status invisible. Either way, your contacts can still call you.

The menu icon to the right of your profile icon with the three vertical dots displays the Skype **Settings menu**. Here you can control how you sign in, receive notifications, and manage privacy functions. If you don't want to see Microsoft targeted ads, uncheck that box.

It's time to add some contacts. Tap the **Add Contacts icon** (the head and shoulders with the + sign) at the top of the screen and search the Skype director for people you know who use Skype. When you find someone you'd like to Skype with, tap **Add to Contacts**.

This will send your contact a message requesting permission to be added to your Skype contacts. If they say yes, you'll be ready to chat.

To chat on Skype, go to your list of contacts and tap the name of the person you want to call. To voice chat, tap the telephone receiver icon below their name; to video chat, tap the video camera icon. You'll hear a ring tone until they answer the call. If you're doing a video chat, be sure to hold your Fire with the front-facing camera pointing toward you. For instant messaging, tap the + icon at the bottom center of the screen and type your message in the box, then tap the arrow icon to send the message.

As you use Skype, you'll see items like Skype Wi-Fi and Skype Credit, which involve spending money. Skype Wi-Fi creates a wireless hotspot for you to use Skype in areas where no wi-fi connection is available, and Skype Calling lets you dial cell phone and land line numbers from your Fire tablet. Both of these services cost money, but as long as you don't add funds to your Skype Credit account with a credit card, Skype will automatically limit you to its free services.

Transferring Photo and Document Files

For transferring an occasional photo or document file between your Fire and another device, an attachment sent through your regular email account works fine. For sharing photo albums and other multiple file collections, you will need something more heavy duty. Here are three ways to transfer data between other devices and your Fire 7.

USB Transfer: To transfer files between your Fire 7 and a computer, plug the full-size end of the micro USB cable into a USB 2.0 port on your computer, and plug the micro end of the cable into your Fire. (Mac users should install Android's free File Transfer app on their computer first, from *www.android.com/filetransfer/*). Once connected, your Fire 7 will display as an external drive icon in your computer's file directory. Click it open, then click the Internal Storage folder, and then the Documents folder to display the files on your Fire's storage drive.

On your computer's hard drive, find the file you want to transfer and simply drag and drop it to the Fire's Documents folder. Eject the Fire device icon from your desktop before unplugging the USB cable. The Fire should automatically detect the type of file you have transferred and will put it in the correct content library. When you open that library, the transferred file will show up under the Device tab. It won't show up in the Cloud tab because the Fire tablet doesn't back up USB transfers to the cloud.

You can also drag and drop files from your Fire 7 to your computer's hard drive with a USB connection. These files can then be transferred to another Kindle or Fire device, or to a smartphone.

Personal Documents Service: This Amazon service lets you send multiple files and large files between your Fire and another device. Unlike a USB transfer, this method stores your data files safely in the Amazon Cloud where you can retrieve them at any time. There is no charge to use this service over Wi-Fi.

Your Fire assigns you a unique email address for using the Personal Documents Service. To find it, tap the Docs app icon in the Apps Grid and swide left to right. Tap *Settings* and tap the *Email icon*. Look for an email address that ends with @kindle.com and jot it down.

Before anyone can send documents to your Amazon email address, you need to pre-approve their email address. Go to your Amazon account via your PC or Mac and choose *Manage Your Content and Devices*, then click the *Settings tab* at the right and scroll down to *Personal Document Settings*. You can then enter the sender's address under Approved Personal Document E-mail List by clicking *Add a New Approved Email Address*. You should also add any of your own email accounts that you plan to use for this service.

Approved senders can send you up to 25 attached documents per email, with the size of each document limited to 50MB before zipping. You must receive and open the email with the Fire email app within 60 days to avoid deletion. Personal Documents Service will store the attachments in your Amazon Cloud library, where you can download them to your Fire 7 at any time with the Docs app in the App Grid. The Docs app organizes your documents into folders, which you open by tapping. Download a single file by tapping its icon, or download multiple files by tapping **Select All** in the upper right corner of the Docs screen and tapping the items you want to download.

You or another sender can speed up the document attachment process on their end by downloading and installing the Send to Kindle application to their computer or Android device. Amazon makes versions of Send to Kindle for PCs, Macs, Android, and specific web browsers. Go to *www.amazon.com/sendtokindle* to download it for your device.

Cloud Drive: For really heavy-duty uploading, you can install the Amazon Cloud Drive desktop application on your computer and upload up to 2GB of data at a time directly to your Amazon Cloud Library account, where it's available for viewing or downloading in the Cloud tab of your Kindle libraries.

To install Cloud Drive on your computer, go to *www.amazon.com/ gp/drive/app-download* and let the site automatically detect which version you need before it presents you with a download. You can also click **Your Cloud Drive** from the drop-down menu under Your Account on the Amazon home screen and install the application from there. Open and install the downloaded file to your hard drive. This application will then let you connect to your Amazon Cloud Drive with your computer so you can upload and download data with a simple drag-and-drop interface.

Alternatively you can just upload your documents, photos and videos straight into your Cloud Drive account via your web browser. Go to the main Amazon Cloud Drive page (*http://www.lyntons.com/ clouddrive*) and instead of clicking on 'Install Cloud Drive' click on **Your Cloud Drive** located at the top right of the page. Clicking the **All Files** option will display a series of content folders. By clicking **upload** you can browse your computer for the relevant content you wish to store.

Working with Documents

Office Suite: The Docs app in your Fire App Grid has some of the same functionality of Microsoft Office. Open the app and tap the + *icon* in the upper right corner of your screen. In the Create pop-up menu, tap *Document, Spreadsheet*, or *Presentation* to create a document to save. There are also several office suite apps for the Fire available in the App Store. Amazon Underground features a free office app called OfficeSuite Pro.

Wireless Printing: The Fire 7 has a robust wireless printing option. From the WPS Office app, your Photo Library, or the Fire email app you can send documents, spreadsheets, emails, images, and presentations to any printer connected to a wi-fi network. The Fire auto-detects all available printers in your network.

Business Productivity: The Fire can be set up to log in to your company's intranet, even if it's set up with Microsoft Exchange. You can the great selection of office productivity apps for the Fire to submit timesheets, expense reports, share and edit documents, and sync your email, contacts, and calendar. Remote VPN access with full encryption is also available from the Settings menu for even greater connectivity and security.

Creating Folders

We like the free ES File Explorer app (*www.lyntons.com/esfile*) for creating and managing folders on our Fire tablet. This nifty little app gives your tablet's storage drive full Windows-like functionality. You can create new folders, select multiple files or folders, drag and drop files and folders, rename them, and - if you dare - delete them. The app also creates shortcuts and has a really well devised search function that sorts by name, date, file size, or category. To install it on your Fire, tap *Apps* in the Category Bar and tap *Store* to go to the App store, where you can use the search box to find it and download it.

Other Useful Image/Document Functions

Sending PDFs: In order to send a PDF document, you will first need to convert it to the AZW format for the Fire 7. But this is simplicity itself as your Fire tablet has a built in converter tool - all you have to do is type the word "convert" into your email's subject line, then attach the PDF and send the message to your Amazon email address (see above).

Taking Screenshots: To capture a screenshot from your Fire at any time, place your fingers on the outside edge of your device and press and hold the **Power** button and the volume-down part of the Volume button at the same time. If you press them both at the exact same time, your Fire tablet will make a shutter clicking sound, fire off a screenshot and save it in your Photos content library. To go to the album, open the **Photos app** in the App Grid.

Saving web images: Tap and hold the web image and an options box will pop up; simply choose **Download Image** and the image will be saved onto your Fire 7.

Sending multiple images: First tap **Photos** in the App Grid to open your Camera Roll. Tap the checkbox icon in the upper right corner next to the camera icon. Select all the images you want to send by tapping on each image. Tap the **Sharing icon** next to the trash can icon. Finally tap the **Email** button to attach all of them to your email. If you want to send a single image, simply tap and hold it, then choose **Email** from the list of options. You can also use this screen to share your images on Twitter and Facebook, or to a Bluetooth device.

9. TROUBLESHOOTING

What to Do If Your Fire 7 Freezes

If your Fire touchscreen completely freezes so you can't force-quit a troublesome app (see **Chapter 4**), then it's time for a hard reset. This should be done without the power adapter or USB cable plugged into the device. Press and hold the Power button for 20 seconds before releasing it, then restart.

If you still experience problems, you can try charging the battery through the USB cable and adapter, unplug, and then do another hard reset followed by a restart.

If a hard reset doesn't solve the problem, go here - *www.lyntons. com/hardreset* on your computer for support.

Lost Passwords or Passcodes

If you lose the password/passcode to either your **Lock Screen** or your **Parental Controls** they can both be reset the same way.

Firstly to reset your **Lock Screen password or PIN**, enter the wrong passcode five times. After the fifth time (the maximum number of times you are allowed to get it wrong in one session) you will be presented with some different options. Choose *Reset Your PIN* and you will be prompted to enter your main Amazon password (the one you used to register your device and you use to login into Amazon). Once you've done this you will be allowed to select and set a new passcode/password.

For your **Parental Control passcode**, again enter a wrong passcode five times and after the fifth attempt choose the *Reset Your Parental Controls Passcode* option and, when prompted, enter you main Amazon password. Then set a new passcode and click *Finish*.

Managing Fire 7 Updates

It's worth remembering that once you've downloaded an app or ebook, you usually have also allowed the developer to send you updated versions. Updates often allow for smoother running of an app, or improved content. These updates are usually automatic and show up in your notifications but from time to time, you might also want to manually check for any updates via the Manage Your Content and Devices (*www.amazon.com/myk*) website. If there are any updates available for either your apps or books you should see a notification next to the title of the product.

Preserving Battery Life

There are a number of useful steps you can take to help conserve the battery life of your Fire, some of which will really depend on how you use it (**see our list below**). But almost everyone should consider doing the following as a matter of course.

Firstly, when you're not using your Fire, but don't necessarily want to turn it completely off, you should use the Sleep Mode option to avoid using up battery power. To activate Sleep Mode, touch the **Power** button: the Fire screen should go black immediately without offering up any command options. If you press the Power button for too long, a message will pop up asking you if you want to shut down - press **Cancel** if the answer is no! To "wake up" your Fire, simply touch the **Power** button again.

You can also choose to set your Fire so that it automatically goes into Sleep Mode after a certain time period of inactivity. Go to **Settings** from the Quick Settings menu or the App Grid, then choose **Power**; here tap on the **Display Settings** option to choose the time delay you want before the Fire goes into Sleep Mode. You can also make sure that **Automatic Smart Suspend** is activated by tapping it so the switch icon displays orange. This disconnects your Fire from all wireless networks if the device is inactive for more than a few minutes.

You can also make sure that apps you're not using are not actually still running - sometimes apps don't fully switch off. Check to see which ones are still running by tapping **Settings** from the Quick Settings menu or the Apps Grid and then **Apps & Games**. Tap **Manage All Applications** and tap **Running** toward the top right of your screen and tap each app to see its status.

An app that has the Force Stop button grayed out is not running, but if isn't grayed out, you can tap it to force quit the app. Use the **Uninstall** button if all else fails, since the app will still be available in your Amazon Cloud library.

Also from Manage All Applications, you can choose which apps you definitely want to run as soon as you turn on your Fire by choosing the **Automatically Launch by Default** option. At the bottom of each app's management screen you'll see the app's permissions on your Fire. Some of these can be quite intrusive, while others prevent your Fire from sleeping so you'll have to charge your battery more often. It's a good idea to know what your apps are doing while you're asleep!

Some other things you can do to prolong the Fire's battery charge include:

1. Using headphones to listen to audio instead of the speakers

2. Turning down screen brightness

3. Turning off the Automatic Brightness option

4. Disabling Wi-Fi and Bluetooth when you aren't using them

5. Avoiding weak Wi-Fi signals as the Fire has to work harder to stay connected

6. Disabling Location-Based Services in the Settings.

7. Checking for email messages less often

8. Opting for Airplane Mode - but remember that this will mean disabling online access

Troubleshooting Wi-Fi Connections

Wi-Fi connection problems can interfere with data transfers and video streaming, or they can cut you off completely. Sometimes they occur if you don't enter the correct password, or if the network is running MAC filtering. MAC-filtered networks require the network administrator to manually add you as a user before you can use their Wi-Fi connection.

A bad Wi-Fi network connection can also be caused by too many users at once, or connectivity problems from the Fire side. Try putting your device to sleep while the power is on by briefly touching the Power button and touching it again to wake it up. You will need to slide the lock button upward on the touchscreen and enter your password or PIN. This process stops and starts the network connection. If this doesn't work, try restarting your Fire.

We have found that different types of Wi-Fi networks work better with the Fire than others. If you just can't connect, try using your computer's Wi-Fi utility to see whether your network is a WPA2 type as we've found that it's the friendliest for connecting to your Fire.

Traveling Overseas with Your Fire

The most important thing to be aware of when traveling outside the United States with your Fire is that many other countries use 220 volt electrical current instead of the 110 volt used in the US. Be sure to purchase a specialized power adapter or quick charger to handle this.

You will want to travel with your power adapter and USB cable, because you probably won't have access to a computer with a USB connection long enough to handle the longer charging times.

Wi-Fi access can be sporadic overseas, so plan to download all the content you will need onto your Fire's storage drive before you leave home.

Extended Warranties

Your new Fire tablet comes with a one-year warranty as a standard feature. If you tap **Shop** in the Category Bar and go to the Kindle store on the Amazon website, you can find some extended warranty options for the Fire serviced by third-party providers. A typical plan provides coverage for 2 years against things like accidents and mechanical or electrical failure. Check whether the warranty includes sending you a replacement Fire immediately after you make a claim, with no deductible or shipping fee, and whether the warranty is transferable.

Where to Go for More Help

The Fire Help Home Page is located at *www.amazon.com/ kindlesupport*, or you can open the Help app from the App Grid. From here you can access one-on-one tech support via phone, e-mail, or chat, or you can read a written user guide and view help videos and tutorials.

Amazon has expanded its on-device tech support, called Mayday, to its Fire tablets. With Screen Sharing, Amazon customer service experts can connect to your Fire tablet to help you navigate by drawing on your screen, showing you how to do something yourself, or doing it for you - whatever works best.

Several Kindle Fire and Fire forums are available on the web that you can access from your browser. Don't believe everything you read in Internet forums, but sometimes they contain hidden gems for troubleshooting your Fire that you can't find anywhere else. Here are some forums that we have found helpful:

- Amazon Customer Forums (*www.lyntons.com/amzforums*)

- Kindle Boards (*www.kindleboards.com/*)

- Mobile Read (*www.mobileread.com/*)

And also be sure to verify that the advice you are reading is specific to the 5th Generation Fire, because most of the support pages for the earlier Kindle Fire models or the Kindle Fire HDX don't apply to the new Fire tablets.

10. FIRE ACCESSORIES

Another thing that makes the Fire so much fun to own is the huge selection of accessories for it. Some of them are must-have items, and some of them are nice-to-have items, but all of them make your experience of owning a Fire just a little bit better. To shop for accessories, start in the Kindle Store on Amazon.

Cases, Stands, Skins and Screen Protectors

A nice case for your Fire is one of the first things you should buy after you purchase the device itself. We prefer a folio-style case that feels like a book when you hold it in your hands. Remember that the case should specifically say that it fits the new Fire 7, because cases for the Kindle Fire's are not interchangeable. Look for a microfiber lining and a secure closure for the case cover so it doesn't accidentally come open. Another good feature is a set of grooves so you can use the case as a stand to make watching videos more comfortable. Be sure to pick a case that doesn't muffle the speakers on the rear of the Fire. Don't forget to pick out a color and fabric you like. Leather cases cost a bit more, but they do look sharp!

If you choose a case that doesn't double as a stand, you can buy a separate stand for video watching. Stands come in a number of designs, including folding travel stands, rigid stands, and stands with adjustable angles.

Lately skins have become all the rage for personalizing your smartphones and tablets. They are essentially a kind of sticker that you attach to your Fire - usually an easy enough process provided you follow the directions that come with the skins. You can buy all kinds of different skin designs for your Fire and there are even websites offering design-your-own custom skins. Make sure that any skin you purchase is compatible with your Fire's specs, and please be aware that these skins are purely decorative and do not provide any protective function at all!

The Kindle Store also sells several types of touchscreen covers for the Fire. You can buy inexpensive adhesive plastic film, or a more substantial anti-glare cover to fit over the screen. A good screen protector will keep your Fire's touchscreen from getting scratched without blocking your touch commands.

A quick search of the Amazon Kindle Store will turn up some nice stylus touch pens to make your swiping and tapping easier. People with big fingers will be especially happy with these! Now that we have a stylus, we use it all the time.

Car Seat Tablet Holders and Mounts

An item which may be of interest to parents, are the different tablet holders designed to attach to the driver or front passenger seats to hold a tablet so that passengers on the back seats can watch whatever you've downloaded onto it. Essentially, it is a clever alternative if your car doesn't have a built-in DVD player and seat screen system - and for some parents it is a lifesaver for those long holiday road trips! In a similar vein, you can also purchase tablet mounts that attach your tablet to the front dashboard area - useful to operate GPS systems or view a pre-downloaded map. With either of these items, double check that they fit the specs of both your car and your new Fire!

Chargers and Adapters

Amazon took the hint from numerous user reviews after the release of the 2012 Kindle Fire HD, which didn't include a charger. The new Fire tablets ship with a 5W adapter to use as a charging device along with a standard USB cable. The adapter charges the Fire in less than 4 hours from 0% to 100% by plugging it into a wall outlet and connecting it to your Fire with the USB cable. The adapter can provide your tablet with continuous AC power, but we have found that it's not very convenient to use our Fire with it tethered to a wall plug!

Another handy power source to have on hand is a car charger that plugs into your vehicle's 12-volt power supply. These often come bundled in a kit with a case and other accessories.

External Devices

The Fire packs a lot of hardware value into its small size, but you can make it even more valuable by plugging in an external device. We list some of the most popular ones below.

Fire Keyboard: This external Bluetooth keyboard - *www.amazon. com/dp/BooKYFWDLU* - is incredibly thin and light so it can go wherever you and your Fire. Don't let its compact size fool you - it has great features, like a built-in trackpad and shortcut keys to frequently performed tasks like checking email and playing music and videos. It even has an Instant Search feature. The Fire Keyboard works with all Fire models.

Headphones: Although the Fire's built-in speakers sound pretty good, a pair of high-end headphones can deliver sound quality good enough to satisfy music lovers, and even a cheap pair of earbuds will keep you from distracting the people around you when you're listening to music or watching videos. The headphone jack is located on the same edge as the power switch of your Fire.

Bluetooth Devices: The Fire's Bluetooth capability allows it to connect wirelessly to a number of external Bluetooth devices. You can purchase headphones, earpieces, microphones, headsets, and external keyboards with Bluetooth capability. These devices will turn your Kindle into something very much like a desktop computer, without a jumble of messy cords and cables.

To set up a Bluetooth connection between your Fire and a wireless device, called "pairing," you need to turn on the external device first and make sure it is within range. Consult your owner's manual for the external device and find out how to set it to pairing mode. Next, pick up your Fire and swipe down from the top of the screen to open the *Quick Actions Menu*. Tap the *Wireless icon* and then tap *Bluetooth*. Tap the *On* button next to enable Bluetooth. Look at the *Available Devices menu* to see if the Fire has detected the Bluetooth signal from the external device. Tap the device name to connect it to your Fire. There might be additional prompts or pairing instructions before the two devices can start "talking" to each other.

The Status Bar at the top of your screen will show the "B" Bluetooth icon when Bluetooth is turned on. Remember that turning off Bluetooth will extend the length of time between battery charges on your Fire.

A Final Reminder About Updates

So you got this far, and we hope you found the book useful - we just want to leave you with a reminder about the FREE Fire app updates for this book. If you want to take advantage of this, sign up for the updates here - *www.lyntons.com/updates*

Don't worry, we hate spam as much as you do so we will never share your details with anyone.

And Finally...

So there you are, you should now have all the tips, tricks and user information you need to get the most out of your new Fire tablet. We are confident that we have covered all the information you could need, but we are only human so if you think we have missed anything important, or could have explained something better, we would love to hear from you. In fact we'd love to hear any comments you have about our book - you can contact us here: *ReachMe@lyntons.com*.

All feedback will be treated in strictest confidence and we will be more than happy to make improvements for our next edition where we can.

Just before we go we would like to ask for your help. As we're sure you know, book reviews on Amazon play a huge part in helping people choose what they should be reading - and it's one of the ways that small independent publishers, like us, can get our voices heard.

So if you've found this book helpful we'd love it if you could take a minute to leave us a review. Thanks you for reading...

31182853R00064

Made in the USA
San Bernardino, CA
03 March 2016